EVERYMAN'S LIBRARY
POCKET POETS

HOPKINS

········

POEMS
AND
PROSE

EVERYMAN'S LIBRARY
POCKET POETS

This selection by Peter Washington first published in
Everyman's Library, 1995
© David Campbell Publishers Ltd., 1995

ISBN 1-85715-721-4

A CIP catalogue record for this book is available from the British Library

Published by David Campbell Publishers Ltd.,
79 Berwick Street, London W1V 3PF

Distributed by Random House (UK) Ltd.,
20 Vauxhall Bridge Road, London SW1V 2SA

Typography by Peter B. Willberg

Typeset by Acc Computing, Queen Camel, Somerset

Printed and bound in Germany by
Mohndruck Graphische Betriebe GmbH, Gütersloh

CONTENTS

GERARD MANLEY HOPKINS

······················

POEMS AND PROSE

SELECTED POEMS

TO R. B.

The fine delight that fathers thought; the strong
Spur, live and lancing like the blowpipe flame,
Breathes once and, quenchèd faster than it came,
Leaves yet the mind a mother of immortal song.

Nine months she then, nay years, nine years she long
Within her wears, bears, cares and combs the same:
The widow of an insight lost she lives, with aim
Now known and hand at work now never wrong.

Sweet fire the sire of muse, my soul needs this;
I want the one rapture of an inspiration.
O then if in my lagging lines you miss

The roll, the rise, the carol, the creation,
My winter world, that scarcely breathes that bliss
Now, yields you, with some sighs, our explanation.

GOD'S GRANDEUR

The world is charged with the grandeur of God.
  It will flame out, like shining from shook foil;
  It gathers to a greatness, like the ooze of oil
Crushed. Why do men then now not reck his rod?
Generations have trod, have trod, have trod;
  And all is seared with trade; bleared, smeared
    with toil;
  And wears man's smudge and shares man's smell:
    the soil
Is bare now, nor can foot feel, being shod.

And for all this, nature is never spent;
  There lives the dearest freshness deep down things;
And though the last lights off the black West went
  Oh, morning, at the brown brink eastward, springs –
Because the Holy Ghost over the bent
  World broods with warm breast and with ah! bright
    wings.

PIED BEAUTY

Glory be to God for dappled things –
   For skies of couple-colour as a brinded cow;
     For rose-moles all in stipple upon trout that swim;
Fresh-firecoal chestnut-falls; finches' wings;
   Landscape plotted and pieced – fold, fallow, and plough;
     And áll trádes, their gear and tackle and trim.

All things counter, original, spare, strange;
   Whatever is fickle, freckled (who knows how?)
     With swift, slow; sweet, sour; adazzle, dim;
He fathers-forth whose beauty is past change:
                   Praise him.

THE SEA AND THE SKYLARK

On ear and ear two noises too old to end
   Trench – right, the tide that ramps against the shore;
   With a flood or a fall, low lull-off or all roar,
Frequenting there while moon shall wear and wend.

Left hand, off land, I hear the lark ascend,
   His rash-fresh re-winded new-skeinèd score
   In crisps of curl off wild winch whirl, and pour
And pelt music, till none's to spill nor spend.

How these two shame this shallow and frail town!
   How ring right out our sordid turbid time,
Being pure! We, life's pride and cared-for crown,

   Have lost that cheer and charm of earth's past prime:
Our make and making break, are breaking, down
   To man's last dust, drain fast towards man's first slime.

THE CAGED SKYLARK

As a dare-gale skylark scanted in a dull cage
   Man's mounting spirit in his bone-house,
     mean house, dwells –
   That bird beyond the remembering his free fells;
This in drudgery, day-labouring-out life's age.

Though aloft on turf or perch or poor low stage,
   Both sing sometimes the sweetest, sweetest spells,
   Yet both droop deadly sómetimes in their cells
Or wring their barriers in bursts of fear or rage.

Not that the sweet-fowl, song-fowl, needs no rest –
Why, hear him, hear him babble and drop down to his nest,
   But his own nest, wild nest, no prison.

Man's spirit will be flesh-bound when found at best,
But uncumberèd: meadow-down is not distressed
   For a rainbow footing it nor he for his bónes rísen.

AS KINGFISHERS CATCH FIRE

As kingfishers catch fire, dragonflies draw flame;
  As tumbled over rim in roundy wells
  Stones ring; like each tucked string tells, each hung bell's
Bow swung finds tongue to fling out broad its name;
Each mortal thing does one thing and the same:
  Deals out that being indoors each one dwells;
  Selves — goes itself; *myself* it speaks and spells,
Crying *What I do is me: for that I came.*

Í say more: the just man justices;
  Keeps gráce: thát keeps all his goings graces;
Acts in God's eye what in God's eye he is —
  Chríst. For Christ plays in ten thousand places,
Lovely in limbs, and lovely in eyes not his
  To the Father through the features of men's faces.

THE WINDHOVER:
To Christ our Lord

I caught this morning morning's minion, king-
    dom of daylight's dauphin, dapple-dawn-drawn
      Falcon, in his riding
    Of the rolling level underneath him steady air,
      and striding
High there, how he rung upon the rein of a wimpling wing
In his ecstasy! then off, off forth on swing,
    As a skate's heel sweeps smooth on a bow-bend:
      the hurl and gliding
    Rebuffed the big wind. My heart in hiding
Stirred for a bird, – the achieve of, the mastery
      of the thing!

Brute beauty and valour and act, oh, air, pride, plume, here
    Buckle! AND the fire that breaks from thee then, a billion
Times told lovelier, more dangerous, O my chevalier!

    No wonder of it: shéer plód makes plough down
      sillion
Shine, and blue-bleak embers, ah my dear,
    Fall, gall themselves, and gash gold-vermilion.

IN THE VALLEY OF THE ELWY

I remember a house where all were good
   To me, God knows, deserving no such thing:
   Comforting smell breathed at very entering,
Fetched fresh, as I suppose, off some sweet wood.

That cordial air made those kind people a hood
   All over, as a bevy of eggs the mothering wing
   Will, or mild nights the new morsels of Spring:
Why, it seemed of course; seemed of right it should.

Lovely the woods, waters, meadows, combes, vales,
All the air things wear that build this world of Wales;
   Only the inmate does not correspond:

God, lover of souls, swaying considerate scales,
Complete thy creature dear O where it fails,
   Being mighty a master, being a father and fond.

PENMAEN POOL
For the Visitors' Book at the Inn

Who long for rest, who look for pleasure
Away from counter, court, or school
O where live well your lease of leisure
But here at, here at Penmaen Pool?

You'll dare the Alp? you'll dart the skiff?
Each sport has here its tackle and tool:
Come, plant the staff by Cadair cliff;
Come, swing the sculls on Penmaen Pool.

What's yonder? Grizzled Dyphwys dim:
The triple-hummocked Giant's Stool,
Hoar messmate, hobs and nobs with him
To halve the bowl of Penmaen Pool.

And all the landscape under survey,
At tranquil turns, by nature's rule,
Rides repeated topsyturvy
In frank, in fairy Penmaen Pool.

And Charles's Wain, the wondrous seven,
And sheep-flock clouds like worlds of wool,
For all they shine so, high in heaven,
Shew brighter shaken in Penmaen Pool.

The Mawddach, how she trips! though throttled
If floodtide teeming thrills her full,
And mazy sands all water-wattled
Waylay her at ebb, past Penmaen Pool.

But what's to see in stormy weather,
When grey showers gather and gusts are cool? –
Why, raindrop-roundels looped together
That lace the face of Penmaen Pool.

Then even in weariest wintry hour
Of New Year's month or surly Yule
Furred snows, charged tuft above tuft, tower
From darksome darksome Penmaen Pool.

And ever, if bound here hardest home,
You've parlour-pastime left and (who'll
Not honour it?) ale like goldy foam
That frocks an oar in Penmaen Pool.

Then come who pine for peace or pleasure
Away from counter, court, or school,
Spend here your measure of time and treasure
And taste the treats of Penmaen Pool.

RIBBLESDALE

Earth, sweet Earth, sweet landscape, with leavès throng
And louchèd low grass, heaven that dost appeal
To, with no tongue to plead, no heart to feel;
That canst but only be, but dost that long –

Thou canst but be, but that thou well dost; strong
Thy plea with him who dealt, nay does now deal,
Thy lovely dale down thus and thus bids reel
Thy river, and o'er gives all to rack or wrong.

And what is Earth's eye, tongue, or heart else, where
Else, but in dear and dogged man? – Ah, the heir
To his own selfbent so bound, so tied to his turn,

To thriftless reave both our rich round world bare
And none reck of world after, this bids wear
Earth brows of such care, care and dear concern.

THE STARLIGHT NIGHT

Look at the stars! look, look up at the skies!
   O look at all the fire-folk sitting in the air!
   The bright boroughs, the circle-citadels there!
Down in dim woods the diamond delves!
      the elves'-eyes!
The grey lawns cold where gold, where quickgold lies!
   Wind-beat whitebeam! airy abeles set on a flare!
   Flake-doves sent floating forth at a farmyard scare! –
Ah well! it is all a purchase, all is a prize.

Buy then! bid then! – What? – Prayer, patience,
      alms, vows.
Look, look: a May-mess, like on orchard boughs!
   Look! March-bloom, like on mealed-with-yellow
      sallows!
These are indeed the barn; withindoors house
The shocks. This piece-bright paling shuts the spouse
   Christ home, Christ and his mother and all his
      hallows.

SPRING

Nothing is so beautiful as Spring –
    When weeds, in wheels, shoot long and lovely
      and lush;
    Thrush's eggs look little low heavens, and thrush
Through the echoing timber does so rinse and wring
The ear, it strikes like lightnings to hear him sing;
    The glassy peartree leaves and blooms, they brush
    The descending blue; that blue is all in a rush
With richness; the racing lambs too have fair their fling.

What is all this juice and all this joy?
    A strain of the earth's sweet being in the beginning
In Eden garden. – Have, get, before it cloy,

    Before it cloud, Christ, lord, and sour with sinning,
Innocent mind and Mayday in girl and boy,
    Most, O maid's child, thy choice and worthy the
      winning.

SPRING AND FALL:
to a young child

Márgarét, áre you gríeving
Over Goldengrove unleaving?
Leáves, líke the things of man, you
With your fresh thoughts care for, can you?
Áh! ás the heart grows older
It will come to such sights colder
By and by, nor spare a sigh
Though worlds of wanwood leafmeal lie;
And yet you *will* weep and know why.
Now no matter, child, the name:
Sórrow's spríngs áre the same.
Nor mouth had, no nor mind, expressed
What heart heard of, ghost guessed:
It ís the blight man was born for,
It is Margaret you mourn for.

HURRAHING IN HARVEST

Summer ends now; now, barbarous in beauty,
        the stooks rise
Around; up above, what wind-walks! what lovely
        behaviour
Of silk-sack clouds! has wilder, wilful-wavier
Meal-drift moulded ever and melted across skies?

I walk, I lift up, I lift up heart, eyes,
Down all that glory in the heavens to glean our
        Saviour;
And, éyes, heárt, what looks, what lips yet gave you a
Rapturous love's greeting of realer, of rounder replies?

And the azurous hung hills are his world-wielding
        shoulder
Majestic – as a stallion stalwart, very-violet-sweet! –
These things, these things were here and but the
        beholder
Wanting; which two when they once meet,
The heart rears wings bold and bolder
And hurls for him, O half hurls earth for him off under
        his feet.

BINSEY POPLARS
felled 1879

My aspens dear, whose airy cages quelled,
Quelled or quenched in leaves the leaping sun,
All felled, felled, are all felled;
   Of a fresh and following folded rank
        Not spared, not one
        That dandled a sandalled
      Shadow that swam or sank
On meadow and river and wind-wandering
   weed-winding bank.

O if we but knew what we do
      When we delve or hew –
  Hack and rack the growing green!
     Since country is so tender
  To touch, her being só slender,
  That, like this sleek and seeing ball
  But a prick will make no eye at all,
     Where we, even where we mean

To mend her we end her,
When we hew or delve:
After-comers cannot guess the beauty been.
Ten or twelve, only ten or twelve
Strokes of havoc únselve
The sweet especial scene,
Rural scene, a rural scene,
Sweet especial rural scene.

INVERSNAID

This darksome burn, horseback brown,
His rollrock highroad roaring down,
In coop and in comb the fleece of his foam
Flutes and low to the lake falls home.

A windpuff-bonnet of fáwn-fróth
Turns and twindles over the broth
Of a pool so pitchblack, féll-frówning,
It rounds and rounds Despair to drowning.

Degged with dew, dappled with dew
Are the groins of the braes that the brook treads
        through,
Wiry heathpacks, flitches of fern,
And the beadbonny ash that sits over the burn.

What would the world be, once bereft
Of wet and of wildness? Let them be left,
O let them be left, wildness and wet;
Long live the weeds and the wilderness yet.

DUNS SCOTUS'S OXFORD

Towery city and branchy between towers;
Cuckoo-echoing, bell-swarmèd, lark-charmèd,
    rook-racked, river-rounded;
The dapple-eared lily below thee; that country and
    town did
Once encounter in, here coped and poisèd powers;

Thou hast a base and brickish skirt there, sours
That neighbour-nature thy grey beauty is grounded
Best in; graceless growth, thou hast confounded
Rural rural keeping – folk, flocks, and flowers.

Yet ah! this air I gather and I release
He lived on; these weeds and waters, these walls are what
He haunted who of all men most sways my spirits
    to peace;

Of realty the rarest-veinèd unraveller; a not
Rivalled insight, be rival Italy or Greece;
Who fired France for Mary without spot.

THE MAY MAGNIFICAT

May is Mary's month, and I
Muse at that and wonder why:
    Her feasts follow reason,
    Dated due to season –

Candlemas, Lady Day;
But the Lady Month, May,
    Why fasten that upon her,
    With a feasting in her honour?

Is it only its being brighter
Than the most are must delight her?
    Is it opportunest
    And flowers finds soonest?

Ask of her, the mighty mother:
Her reply puts this other
    Question: What is Spring? –
    Growth in everything –

Flesh and fleece, fur and feather,
Grass and greenworld all together;
    Star-eyed strawberry-breasted
    Throstle above her nested

Cluster of bugle blue eggs thin
Forms and warms the life within;
    And bird and blossom swell
    In sod or sheath or shell.

All things rising, all things sizing
Mary sees, sympathising
    With that world of good,
    Nature's motherhood.

Their magnifying of each its kind
With delight calls to mind
    How she did in her stored
    Magnify the Lord.

Well but there was more than this:
Spring's universal bliss
    Much, had much to say
    To offering Mary May.

When drop-of-blood-and-foam-dapple
Bloom lights the orchard-apple
    And thicket and thorp are merry
    With silver-surfèd cherry

And azuring-over greybell makes
Wood banks and brakes wash wet like lakes
    And magic cuckoocall
    Caps, clears, and clinches all –

This ecstasy all through mothering earth
Tells Mary her mirth till Christ's birth
    To remember and exultation
    In God who was her salvation.

THE BLESSED VIRGIN
COMPARED TO THE
AIR WE BREATHE

Wild air, world-mothering air,
Nestling me everywhere,
That each eyelash or hair
Girdles; goes home betwixt
The fleeciest, frailest-flixed
Snowflake; that's fairly mixed
With, riddles, and is rife
In every least thing's life;
This needful, never spent,
And nursing element;
My more than meat and drink,
My meal at every wink;
This air, which, by life's law,
My lung must draw and draw
Now but to breathe its praise,
Minds me in many ways
Of her who not only
Gave God's infinity
Dwindled to infancy
Welcome in womb and breast,
Birth, milk, and all the rest
But mothers each new grace
That does now reach our race –

Mary Immaculate,
Merely a woman, yet
Whose presence, power is
Great as no goddess's
Was deemèd, dreamèd; who
This one work has to do –
Let all God's glory through,
God's glory which would go
Through her and from her flow
Off, and no way but so.

    I say that we are wound
With mercy round and round
As if with air: the same
Is Mary, more by name.
She, wild web, wondrous robe,
Mantles the guilty globe,
Since God has let dispense
Her prayers his providence:
Nay, more than almoner,
The sweet alms' self is her
And men are meant to share
Her life as life does air.

    If I have understood,
She holds high motherhood
Towards all our ghostly good
And plays in grace her part
About man's beating heart,

Laying, like air's fine flood,
The deathdance in his blood;
Yet no part but what will
Be Christ our Saviour still.
Of her flesh he took flesh:
He does take fresh and fresh,
Though much the mystery how,
Not flesh but spirit now
And makes, O marvellous!
New Nazareths in us,
Where she shall yet conceive
Him, morning, noon, and eve;
New Bethlems, and he born
There, evening, noon, and morn –
Bethlem or Nazareth,
Men here may draw like breath
More Christ and baffle death;
Who, born so, comes to be
New self and nobler me
In each one and each one
More makes, when all is done,
Both God's and Mary's Son.

    Again, look overhead
How air is azurèd;
O how! Nay do but stand
Where you can lift your hand
Skywards: rich, rich it laps

Round the four fingergaps.
Yet such a sapphire-shot,
Charged, steepèd sky will not
Stain light. Yea, mark you this:
It does no prejudice.
The glass-blue days are those
When every colour glows,
Each shape and shadow shows.
Blue be it: this blue heaven
The seven or seven times seven
Hued sunbeam will transmit
Perfect, not alter it.
Or if there does some soft,
On things aloof, aloft,
Bloom breathe, that one breath more
Earth is the fairer for.
Whereas did air not make
This bath of blue and slake
His fire, the sun would shake,
A blear and blinding ball
With blackness bound, and all
The thick stars round him roll
Flashing like flecks of coal,
Quartz-fret, or sparks of salt,
In grimy vasty vault.
　　So God was god of old:
A mother came to mould

Those limbs like ours which are
What must make our daystar
Much dearer to mankind;
Whose glory bare would blind
Or less would win man's mind.
Through her we may see him
Made sweeter, not made dim,
And her hand leaves his light
Sifted to suit our sight.

      Be thou then, O thou dear
Mother, my atmosphere;
My happier world, wherein
To wend and meet no sin;
Above me, round me lie
Fronting my froward eye
With sweet and scarless sky;
Stir in my ears, speak there
Of God's love, O live air,
Of patience, penance, prayer:
World-mothering air, air wild,
Wound with thee, in thee isled,
Fold home, fast fold thy child.

AD MARIAM

When a sister, born for each strong month-brother,
   Spring's one daughter, the sweet child May,
Lies in the breast of the young year-mother
   With light on her face like the waves at play,
Man from the lips of him speaketh and saith,
At the touch of her wandering wondering breath
Warm on his brow: lo! where is another
   Fairer than this one to brighten our day?

We have suffered the sons of Winter in sorrow
   And been in their ruinous reigns oppressed,
And fain in the springtime surcease would borrow
   From all the pain of the past's unrest;
And May has come, hair-bound in flowers,
With eyes that smile thro' the tears of the hours,
With joy for to-day and hope for to-morrow
   And the promise of Summer within her breast!

And we that joy in this month joy-laden,
    The gladdest thing that our eyes have seen,
Oh thou, proud mother and much proud maiden –
    Maid yet mother as May hath been –
To thee we tender the beauties all
Of the month by men called virginal.
And, where thou dwellest in deep-groved Aidenn,
    Salute thee, mother, the maid-month's Queen!

For thou, as she, wert the one fair daughter
    That came when a line of kings did cease,
Princes strong for the sword and slaughter,
    That, warring, wasted the land's increase,
And like the storm-months smote the earth
Till a maid in David's house had birth,
That was unto Judah as May, and brought her
    A son for King, whose name was peace.

Wherefore we love thee, wherefore we sing to thee,
    We, all we, thro' the length of our days,
The praise of the lips and the hearts of us bring to thee,
    Thee, oh maiden, most worthy of praise;
For lips and hearts they belong to thee
Who to us are as dew unto grass and tree,
For the fallen rise and the stricken spring to thee,
    Thee, May-hope of our darkened ways!

NEW READINGS

Although the letter said
On thistles that men look not grapes to gather,
   I read the story rather
How soldiers platting thorns around CHRIST'S Head
   Grapes grew and drops of wine were shed.

Though when the sower sowed,
The wingèd fowls took part, part fell in thorn
   And never turned to corn,
Part found no root upon the flinty road, –
   CHRIST at all hazards fruit hath shewed.

From wastes of rock He brings
Food for five thousand: on the thorns He shed
   Grains from His drooping Head;
And would not have that legion of winged things
   Bear Him to heaven on easeful wings.

HEAVEN-HAVEN
A nun takes the veil

I have desired to go
    Where springs not fail,
To fields where flies no sharp and sided hail
    And a few lilies blow.

And I have asked to be
    Where no storms come,
Where the green swell is in the havens dumb,
    And out of the swing of the sea.

THE HALF-WAY HOUSE

Love I was shewn upon the mountain-side
And bid to catch Him ere the drop of day.
See, Love, I creep and Thou on wings dost ride:
Love, it is evening now and Thou away;
Love, it grows darker here and Thou art above;
Love, come down to me if Thy name be Love.

My national old Egyptian reed gave way;
I took of vine a cross-barred rod or rood.
Then next I hungered: Love when here, they say,
Or once or never took Love's proper food;
But I must yield the chase, or rest and eat. –
Peace and food cheered me where four rough ways meet.

Hear yet my paradox: Love, when all is given,
To see Thee I must see Thee, to love, love;
I must o'ertake Thee at once and under heaven
If I shall overtake Thee at last above.
You have your wish; enter these walls, one said:
He is with you in the breaking of the bread.

THE HABIT OF PERFECTION

Elected Silence, sing to me
And beat upon my whorlèd ear,
Pipe me to pastures still and be
The music that I care to hear.

Shape nothing, lips; be lovely-dumb:
It is the shut, the curfew sent
From there where all surrenders come
Which only makes you eloquent.

Be shellèd, eyes, with double dark
And find the uncreated light:
This ruck and reel which you remark
Coils, keeps, and teases simple sight.

Palate, the hutch of tasty lust,
Desire not to be rinsed with wine:
The can must be so sweet, the crust
So fresh that come in fasts divine!

Nostrils, your careless breath that spend
Upon the stir and keep of pride,
What relish shall the censers send
Along the sanctuary side!

O feel-of-primrose hands, O feet
That want the yield of plushy sward,
But you shall walk the golden street
And you unhouse and house the Lord.

And, Poverty, be thou the bride
And now the marriage feast begun,
And lily-coloured clothes provide
Your spouse not laboured-at nor spun.

NONDUM

'Verily Thou art a God that hidest Thyself.'
ISAIAH xlv. 15.

God, though to Thee our psalm we raise
No answering voice comes from the skies;
To Thee the trembling sinner prays
But no forgiving voice replies;
Our prayer seems lost in desert ways,
Our hymn in the vast silence dies.

We see the glories of the earth
But not the hand that wrought them all:
Night to a myriad worlds gives birth,
Yet like a lighted empty hall
Where stands no host at door or hearth
Vacant creation's lamps appal.

We guess; we clothe Thee, unseen King,
With attributes we deem are meet;
Each in his own imagining
Sets up a shadow in Thy seat;
Yet know not how our gifts to bring,
Where seek Thee with unsandalled feet.

And still th'unbroken silence broods
While ages and while aeons run,
As erst upon chaotic floods
The Spirit hovered ere the sun
Had called the seasons' changeful moods
And life's first germs from death had won.

And still th'abysses infinite
Surround the peak from which we gaze.
Deep calls to deep, and blackest night
Giddies the soul with blinding daze
That dares to cast its searching sight
On being's dread and vacant maze.

And Thou art silent, whilst Thy world
Contends about its many creeds
And hosts confront with flags unfurled
And zeal is flushed and pity bleeds
And truth is heard, with tears impearled,
A moaning voice among the reeds.

My hand upon my lips I lay;
The breast's desponding sob I quell;
I move along life's tomb-decked way
And listen to the passing bell
Summoning men from speechless day
To death's more silent, darker spell.

Oh! till Thou givest that sense beyond,
To show Thee that Thou art, and near,
Let patience with her chastening wand
Dispel the doubt and dry the tear;
And lead me child-like by the hand
If still in darkness not in fear.

Speak! whisper to my watching heart
One word – as when a mother speaks
Soft, when she sees her infant start,
Till dimpled joy steals o'er its cheeks.
Then, to behold Thee as Thou art,
I'll wait till morn eternal breaks.

HENRY PURCELL

*The poet wishes well to the divine genius of Purcell and
praises him that, whereas other musicians have given
utterance to the moods of man's mind, he has, beyond that,
uttered in notes the very make and species of man as
created both in him and in all men generally.*

Have fair fallen, O fair, fair have fallen, so dear
To me, so arch-especial a spirit as heaves in
    Henry Purcell,
An age is now since passed, since parted; with the reversal
    Of the outward sentence low lays him,
    listed to a heresy, here.

Not mood in him nor meaning, proud fire
    or sacred fear,
Or love or pity or all that sweet notes not his
    might nursle:
It is the forgèd feature finds me; it is the rehearsal
Of own, of abrúpt sélf there so thrusts on, so throngs
    the ear.

Let him oh! with his air of angels then lift me, lay me!
    only I'll
Have an eye to the sakes of him, quaint moonmarks,
    to his pelted plumage under
Wings: so some great stormfowl, whenever he has
    walked his while

The thunder-purple seabeach plumèd
    purple-of-thunder,
If a wuthering of his palmy snow-pinions scatter
    a colossal smile
Off him, but meaning motion fans fresh our wits
    with wonder.

In honour of
ST. ALPHONSUS RODRIGUEZ
Laybrother of the Society of Jesus

Honour is flashed off exploit, so we say;
And those strokes once that gashed flesh or galled
    shield
Should tongue that time now, trumpet now that field,
And, on the fighter, forge his glorious day.
On Christ they do and on the martyr may;
But be the war within, the brand we wield
Unseen, the heroic breast not outward-steeled,
Earth hears no hurtle then from fiercest fray.
Yet God (that hews mountain and continent,
Earth, all, out; who, with trickling increment,
Veins violets and tall trees makes more and more)
Could crowd career with conquest while there went
Those years and years by of world without event
That in Majorca Alfonso watched the door.

THE LANTERN OUT OF DOORS

Sometimes a lantern moves along the night,
   That interests our eyes. And who goes there?
   I think; where from and bound, I wonder, where,
With, all down darkness wide, his wading light?

Men go by me whom either beauty bright
   In mould or mind or what not else makes rare:
   They rain against our much-thick and marsh air
Rich beams, till death or distance buys them quite.

Death or distance soon consumes them: wind
   What most I may eye after, be in at the end
I cannot, and out of sight is out of mind.

Christ minds: Christ's interest, what to avow or amend
   There, éyes them, heart wánts, care haúnts, foot
      fóllows kínd,
Their ránsom, théir rescue, ánd first, fást, last friénd.

THE CANDLE INDOORS

Some candle clear burns somewhere I come by.
I muse at how its being puts blissful back
With yellowy moisture mild night's blear-all black,
Or to-fro tender trambeams truckle at the eye.

By that window what task what fingers ply,
I plod wondering, a-wanting, just for lack
Of answer the eagerer a-wanting Jessy or Jack
There/God to aggrándise, God to glorify. –

Come you indoors, come home; your fading fire
Mend first and vital candle in close heart's vault:
You there are master, do your own desire;

What hinders? Are you beam-blind, yet to a fault
In a neighbour deft-handed? are you that liar
And, cast by conscience out, spendsavour salt?

TOM'S GARLAND:
upon the Unemployed

Tom – garlanded with squat and surly steel
Tom; then Tom's fallowbootfellow piles pick
By him and rips out rockfire homeforth – sturdy Dick;
Tom Heart-at-ease, Tom Navvy: he is all for his meal
Sure, 's bed now. Low be it: lustily he his low lot (feel
That ne'er need hunger, Tom; Tom seldom sick,
Seldomer heartsore; that treads through,
      prickproof, thick
Thousands of thorns, thoughts) swings though.
      Commonweal
Little Í reck ho! lacklevel in, if all had bread:
What! Country is honour enough in all us – lordly head,
With heaven's lights high hung round, or,
      mother-ground
That mammocks, mighty foot. But nó way sped,
Nor mind nor mainstrength; gold go garlanded
With, perilous, O nó; nor yet plod safe shod sound;
         Undenizened, beyond bound
Of earth's glory, earth's ease, all; no one, nowhere,
In wide the world's weal; rare gold, bold steel, bare
        In both; care, but share care –
This, by Despair, bred Hangdog dull; by Rage,
Manwolf, worse; and their packs infest the age.

HARRY PLOUGHMAN

Hard as hurdle arms, with a broth of goldish flue
Breathed round; the rack of ribs; the scooped flank; lank
Rope-over thigh; knee-nave; and barrelled shank –
     Head and foot, shoulder and shank –
By a grey eye's heed steered well, one crew, fall to;
Stand at stress. Each limb's barrowy brawn, his thew
That onewhere curded, onewhere sucked or sank –
     Soared ór sánk –,
Though as a beechbole firm, finds his, as at a rollcall, rank
And features, in flesh, what deed he each must do –
     His sinew-service where do.

He leans to it, Harry bends, look. Back, elbow, and
    liquid waist
In him, all quail to the wallowing o' the plough.
    'S check crimsons; curls
Wag or crossbridle, in a wind lifted, windlaced –
     See his wind- lilylocks -laced;
Churlsgrace, too, child of Amansstrength, how it
    hangs or hurls
Them – broad in bluff hide his frowning feet lashed!
    raced
With, along them, cragiron under and cold furls –
     With-a-fountain's shining-shot furls.

THE BUGLER'S FIRST COMMUNION

A bugler boy from barrack (it is over the hill
There) – boy bugler, born, he tells me, of Irish
       Mother to an English sire (he
Shares their best gifts surely, fall how things will),

This very very day came down to us after a boon he on
My late being there begged of me, overflowing
       Boon in my bestowing,
Came, I say, this day to it – to a First Communion.

Here he knelt then ín regimental red.
Forth Christ from cupboard fetched, how fain I of feet
       To his youngster take his treat!
Low-latched in leaf-light housel his too huge godhead.

There! and your sweetest sendings, ah divine,
By it, heavens, befall him! as a heart Christ's darling,
    dauntless;
       Tongue true, vaunt- and tauntless;
Breathing bloom of a chastity in mansex fine.

Frowning and forefending angel-warder
Squander the hell-rook ranks sally to molest him;
       March, kind comrade, abreast him;
Dress his days to a dexterous and starlight order.

How it dóes my heart good, visiting at that bleak hill,
When limber liquid youth, that to all I teach
       Yields tender as a pushed peach,
Hies headstrong to its wellbeing of a self-wise self-will!

Then though I should tread tufts of consolation
Dáys áfter, só I in a sort deserve to
       And do serve God to serve to
Just such slips of soldiery Christ's royal ration.

Nothing élse is like it, no, not all so strains
Us: fresh youth fretted in a bloomfall all portending
       That sweet's sweeter ending;
Realm both Christ is heir to and thére réigns.

O now well work that sealing sacred ointment!
O for now charms, arms, what bans off bad
       And locks love ever in a lad!
Let mé though see no more of him, and not
   disappointment

Those sweet hopes quell whose least me quickenings lift,
In scarlet or somewhere of some day seeing
       That brow and bead of being,
An our day's God's own Galahad. Though this child's drift

Seems by a divíne doom chánnelled, nor do I cry
Disaster there; but may he not rankle and roam
      In backwheels though bound home? –
That left to the Lord of the Eucharist, I here lie by;

Recorded only, I have put my lips on pleas
Would brandle adamantine heaven with ride and jar, did
      Prayer go disregarded:
Forward-like, but however, and like favourable heaven
    heard these.

BROTHERS

How lovely the elder brother's
Life all laced in the other's,
Lóve-laced! – what once I well
Witnessed; so fortune fell.
When Shrovetide, two years gone,
Our boys' plays brought on
Part was picked for John,
Young Jóhn; then fear, then joy
Ran revel in the elder boy.
Now the night come; all
Our company thronged the hall;
Henry, by the wall,
Beckoned me beside him:
I came where called, and eyed him
By meanwhiles; making mý play
Turn most on tender byplay.
For, wrung all on love's rack,
My lad, and lost in Jack,
Smiled, blushed, and bit his lip;
Or drove, with a diver's dip,
Clutched hands through claspèd knees;
And many a mark like these,
Told tales with what heart's stress
He hung on the imp's success.

Now the other was bráss-bóld:
Hé had no work to hold
His heart up at the strain;
Nay, roguish ran the vein.
Two tedious acts were past;
Jack's call and cue at last;
When Henry, heart-forsook,
Dropped eyes and dared not look.
Thére! the háll rúng!
Dog, he did give tongue!
But Harry – in his hands he has flung
His tear-tricked cheeks of flame
For fond love and for shame.

    Ah Nature, framed in fault,
There's comfort then, there's salt;
Nature, bad, base, and blind,
Dearly thou canst be kind;
There dearly thén, deárly,
Dearly thou canst be kind.

THE SOLDIER

Yes. Whý do we áll, seeing of a soldier, bless him? bless
Our redcoats, our tars? Both these being, the greater part,
But frail clay, nay but foul clay. Here it is: the heart,
Since, proud, it calls the calling manly, gives a guess
That, hopes that, makesbelieve, the men must be no less;
It fancies, feigns, deems, dears the artist after his art;
And fain will find as sterling all as all is smart,
And scarlet wear the spirit of wár thére express.
Mark Christ our King. He knows war, served this
    soldiering through;
He of all can reeve a rope best. There he bides in bliss
Now, and séeing somewhére some mán do all that man
    can do,
For love he leans forth, needs his neck must fall on, kiss,
And cry 'O Christ-done deed! So God-made-flesh does too:
Were I come o'er again' cries Christ 'it should be this'.

FELIX RANDAL

Felix Randal the farrier, O is he dead then?
    my duty all ended,
Who have watched his mould of man, big-boned
    and hardy-handsome
Pining, pining, till time when reason rambled in it
    and some
Fatal four disorders, fleshed there, all contended?

Sickness broke him. Impatient, he cursed at first,
    but mended
Being anointed and all; though a heavenlier heart
    began some
Months earlier, since I had our sweet reprieve
    and ransom
Tendered to him. Ah well, God rest him all road
    ever he offended!

This seeing the sick endears them to us,
    us too it endears.
My tongue had taught thee comfort, touch had
    quenched thy tears,
Thy tears that touched my heart, child, Felix,
    poor Felix Randal;

How far from then forethought of, all thy more
        boisterous years,
When thou at the random grim forge, powerful
        amidst peers,
Didst fettle for the great grey drayhorse
        his bright and battering sandal!

WHERE ART THOU FRIEND

Where art thou friend, whom I shall never see,
Conceiving whom I must conceive amiss?
Or sunder'd from my sight in the age that is
Or far-off promise of a time to be;
Thou who canst best accept the certainty
That thou hadst borne proportion in my bliss,
That likest in me either that or this, –
Oh! even for the weakness of the plea
That I have taken to plead with, – if the sound
Of God's dear pleadings have as yet not moved thee, –
And for those virtues I in thee have found,
Who say that had I known I had approved thee, –
For these, make all the virtues to abound, –
No, but for Christ who hath foreknown and loved thee.

SEE HOW SPRING OPENS

See how Spring opens with disabling cold,
And hunting winds and the long-lying snow.
Is it a wonder if the buds are slow?
Or where is strength to make the leaf unfold?
Chilling remembrance of my days of old
Afflicts no less, what yet I hope may blow,
That seed which the good sower once did sow,
So loading with obstruction that threshold
Which should ere now have led my feet to the field.
It is the waste done in unreticent youth
Which makes so small the promise of that yield
That I may win with late-learnt skill uncouth
From furrows of the poor and stinting weald.
Therefore how bitter, and learnt how late, the truth!

MYSELF UNHOLY

Myself unholy, from myself unholy
To the sweet living of my friends I look –
Eye-greeting doves bright-counter to the rook,
Fresh brooks to salt sand-teasing waters shoaly: –
And they are purer, but alas! not solely
The unquestion'd readings of a blotless book.
And so my trust, confusèd, struck, and shook
Yields to the sultry siege of melancholy.
He has a sin of mine, he its near brother;
Knowing them well I can but see the fall.
This fault in one I found, that in another:
And so, though each have one while I have all,
No *better* serves me now, save *best*; no other
Save Christ: to Christ I look, on Christ I call.

NO WORST

No worst, there is none. Pitched past pitch of grief,
More pangs will, schooled at forepangs, wilder wring.
Comforter, where, where is your comforting?
Mary, mother of us, where is your relief?
My cries heave, herds-long; huddle in a main, a chief-
woe, world-sorrow; on an age-old anvil wince and sing –
Then lull, then leave off. Fury had shrieked 'No ling-
ering! Let me be fell: force I must be brief'.
O the mind, mind has mountains; cliffs of fall
Frightful, sheer, no-man-fathomed. Hold them cheap
May who ne'er hung there. Nor does long our small
Durance deal with that steep or deep. Here! creep,
Wretch, under a comfort serves in a whirlwind: all
Life death does end and each day dies with sleep.

TO SEEM THE STRANGER

To seem the stranger lies my lot, my life
Among strangers. Father and mother dear,
Brothers and sisters are in Christ not near
And he my peace/my parting, sword and strife.

England, whose honour O all my heart woos, wife
To my creating thought, would neither hear
Me, were I pleading, plead nor do I: I wear-
y of idle a being but by where wars are rife.

I am in Ireland now; now I am at a thírd
Remove. Not but in all removes I can
Kind love both give and get. Only what word

Wisest my heart breeds dark heaven's baffling ban
Bars or hell's spell thwarts. This to hoard unheard,
Heard unheeded, leaves me a lonely began.

THOU ART INDEED JUST

Justus quidem tu es, Domine, si disputem tecum;
verumtamen justa loquar ad te: Quare via impiorum
prosperatur? &c.

Thou art indeed just, Lord, if I contend
With thee; but, sir, so what I plead is just.
Why do sinners' ways prosper? and why must
Disappointment all I endeavour end?

Wert thou my enemy, O thou my friend,
How wouldst thou worse, I wonder, than thou dost
Defeat, thwart me? Oh, the sots and thralls of lust
Do in spare hours more thrive than I that spend,

Sir, life upon thy cause. See, banks and brakes
Now, leavèd how thick! lacèd they are again
With fretty chervil, look, and fresh wind shakes

Them; birds build – but not I build; no, but strain,
Time's eunuch, and not breed one work that wakes.
Mine, O thou lord of life, send my roots rain.

I WAKE AND FEEL

I wake and feel the fell of dark, not day.
What hours, O what black hoürs we have spent
This night! what sights you, heart, saw; ways you went!
And more must, in yet longer light's delay.

With witness I speak this. But where I say
Hours I mean years, mean life. And my lament
Is cries countless, cries like dead letters sent
To dearest him that lives alas! away.

I am gall, I am heartburn. God's most deep decree
Bitter would have me taste: my taste was me;
Bones built in me, flesh filled, blood brimmed the curse.

Selfyeast of spirit a dull dough sours. I see
The lost are like this, and their scourge to be
As I am mine, their sweating selves; but worse.

CARRION COMFORT

Not, I'll not, carrion comfort, Despair, not feast on thee;
Not untwist – slack they may be – these last strands of man
In me ór, most weary, cry *I can no more*. I can;
Can something, hope, wish day come, not choose not to be.

But ah, but O thou terrible, why wouldst thou rude on me
Thy wring-world right foot rock? lay a lionlimb
    against me? scan
With darksome devouring eyes my bruisèd bones? and fan,
O in turns of tempest, me heaped there; me frantic to
    avoid thee and flee?

Why? That my chaff might fly; my grain lie, sheer and
    clear.
Nay in all that toil, that coil, since (seems) I kissed the rod,
Hand rather, my heart lo! lapped strength, stole joy,
    would laugh, chéer.
Cheer whom though? The hero whose heaven-
    handling flung me, fóot tród
Me? or me that fought him? O which one? is it each one?
    That night, that year
Of now done darkness I wretch lay wrestling with (my
    God!) my God.

THE SHEPHERD'S BROW

The shepherd's brow, fronting forked lightning, owns
The horror and the havoc and the glory
Of it. Angels fall, they are towers, from heaven – a story
Of just, majestical, and giant groans.
But man – we, scaffold of score brittle bones;
Who breathe, from groundlong babyhood to hoary
Age gasp; whose breath is our *memento mori* –
What bass is *our* viol for tragic tones?
He! Hand to mouth he lives, and voids with shame;
And, blazoned in however bold the name,
Man Jack the man is, just; his mate a hussy.
And I that die these deaths, that feed this flame,
That . . . in smooth spoons spy life's masque mirrored: tame
My tempests there, my fire and fever fussy.

PATIENCE

Patience, hard thing! the hard thing but to pray,
But bid for, Patience is! Patience who asks
Wants war, wants wounds; weary his times, his tasks;
To do without, take tosses, and obey.

Rare patience roots in these, and, these away,
Nowhere. Natural heart's ivy, Patience masks
Our ruins of wrecked past purpose. There she basks
Purple eyes and seas of liquid leaves all day.

We hear our hearts grate on themselves: it kills
To bruise them dearer. Yet the rebellious wills
Of us we do bid God bend to him even so.

And where is he who more and more distills
Delicious kindness? – He is patient. Patience fills
His crisp combs, and that comes those ways we know.

PEACE

When will you ever, Peace, wild wooddove, shy wings
    shut,
Your round me roaming end, and under be my boughs?
When, when, Peace, will you, Peace? I'll not play
    hypocrite

To own my heart: I yield you do come sometimes; but
That piecemeal peace is poor peace. What pure peace
    allows
Alarms of wars, the daunting wars, the death of it?

O surely, reaving Peace, my Lord should leave in lieu
Some good! And so he does leave Patience exquisite,
That plumes to Peace thereafter. And when Peace here
    does house
He comes with work to do, he does not come to coo,
               He comes to brood and sit.

MY OWN HEART

My own heart let me more have pity on; let
Me live to my sad self hereafter kind,
Charitable; not live this tormented mind
With this tormented mind tormenting yet.

I cast for comfort I can no more get
By groping round my comfortless, than blind
Eyes in their dark can day or thirst can find
Thirst's all-in-all in all a world of wet.

Soul, self; come, poor Jackself, I do advise
You, jaded, let be; call off thoughts awhile
Elsewhere; leave comfort root-room; let joy size

At God knows when to God knows what; whose smile
's not wrung, see you; unforeseen times rather – as skies
Betweenpie mountains – lights a lovely mile.

ANDROMEDA

Now Time's Andromeda on this rock rude,
With not her either beauty's equal or
Her injury's, looks off by both horns of shore,
Her flower, her piece of being, doomed dragon food.

Time past she has been attempted and pursued
By many blows and banes; but now hears roar
A wilder beast from West than all were, more
Rife in her wrongs, more lawless, and more lewd.

Her Perseus linger and leave her tó her extremes? –
Pillowy air he treads a time and hangs
His thoughts on her, forsaken that she seems,

All while her patience, morselled into pangs,
Mounts; then to alight disarming, no one dreams,
With Gorgon's gear and barebill/thongs and fangs.

SPELT FROM SYBIL'S LEAVES

Earnest, earthless, equal, attuneable, ⎪vaulty,
    voluminous, . . . stupendous
Evening strains to be tíme's vást, ⎪womb-of-all, home-
    of-all, hearse-of-all night.
Her fond yellow hornlight wound to the west, ⎪her wild
    hollow hoarlight hung to the height
Waste; her earliest stars, earlstars, ⎪stárs principal,
    overbend us,
Fíre-féaturing heaven. For earth ⎪her being has
    unbound; her dapple is at an end, as-
tray or aswarm, all throughther, in throngs; ⎪self ín self
    steepèd and páshed – qúite
Disremembering, dísmémbering ⎪áll now. Heart, you
    round me right
With: Óur évening is over us; óur night ⎪whélms,
    whélms, ánd will end us.
Only the beakleaved boughs dragonish ⎪damask the
    tool-smooth bleak light; black,

Ever so black on it. Óur tale, O óur oracle! | Lét life,
    wáned, ah lét life wind
Off hér once skéined stained véined varíety | upon, áll
    on twó spools; párt, pen, páck
Now her áll in twó flocks, twó folds – black, white; |
    right, wrong; reckon but, reck but, mind
But thése two; wáre of a wórld where bút these | twó
    tell, each off the óther; of a rack
Where, selfwrung, selfstrung, sheathe- and shelterless,
    | thóughts agaínst thoughts ín groans grínd.

THE LEADEN ECHO AND
THE GOLDEN ECHO
(*Maidens' song from St. Winefred's Well*)

THE LEADEN ECHO

How to kéep – is there ány any, is there none such,
      nowhere known some, bow or brooch or braid or
      brace, láce, latch or catch or key to keep
Back beauty, keep it, beauty, beauty, beauty, . . . from
      vanishing away?
Ó is there no frowning of these wrinkles, rankèd
      wrinkles deep,
Dówn? no waving off of these most mournful
      messengers, still messengers, sad and stealing
      messengers of grey? –
No there's none, there's none, O no there's none,
Nor can you long be, what you now are, called fair,
Do what you may do, what, do what you may,
And wisdom is early to despair:
Be beginning; since, no, nothing can be done
To keep at bay
Age and age's evils, hoar hair,
Ruck and wrinkle, drooping, dying, death's worst,
      winding sheets, tombs and worms and tumbling
      to decay;
So be beginning, be beginning to despair.
O there's none; no no no there's none:

Be beginning to despair, to despair,
Despair, despair, despair, despair.

THE GOLDEN ECHO   Spare!
There ís one, yes I have one (Hush there!),
Only not within seeing of the sun.
Not within the singeing of the strong sun,
Tall sun's tingeing, or treacherous the tainting of the
        earth's air,
Somewhere elsewhere there is ah well where! one,
Óne. Yes I cán tell such a key, I dó know such a place,
Where whatever's prizèd and passes of us, everything
        that's fresh and fast flying of us, seems to us sweet
            of us and swiftly away with, done away with,
                undone,
Undone, done with, soon done with, and yet dearly and
        dangerously sweet
Of us, the wimpled-water-dimpled, not-by-morning-
        matchèd face,
The flower of beauty, fleece of beauty, too too apt to,
        ah! to fleet,
Never fleets móre, fastened with the tenderest truth
To its own best being and its loveliness of youth: it is
        an everlastingness of, O it is an all youth!
Come then, your ways and airs and looks, locks,
        maidengear, gallantry and gaiety and grace,
Winning ways, airs innocent, maiden manners, sweet

looks, loose locks, long locks, lovelocks, gaygear,
    going gallant, girlgrace –
Resign them, sign them, seal them, send them, motion
    them with breath,
And with sighs soaring, soaring síghs, deliver
Them; beauty-in-the-ghost, deliver it, early now, long
    before death
Give beauty back, beauty, beauty, beauty, back to God,
    beauty's self and beauty's giver.
See; not a hair is, not an eyelash, not the least lash lost;
    every hair
Is, hair of the head, numbered.
Nay, what we had lighthanded left in surly the mere
    mould
Will have waked and have waxed and have walked
    with the wind what while we slept,
This side, that side hurling a heavyheaded hundredfold
What while we, while we slumbered.
O then, weary then whý should we tread? O why are
    we so haggard at the heart, so care-coiled,
    care-killed, so fagged, so fashed, so cogged, so
    cumbered,
When the thing we freely fórfeit is kept with fonder a
    care,
Fonder a care kept than we could have kept it, kept
Far with fonder a care (and we, we should have lost it)
    finer, fonder

A care kept. – Where kept? do but tell us where kept,
        where. –
Yonder. – What high as that! We follow, now we follow. –
        Yonder, yes yonder, yonder,
Yonder.

TO WHAT SERVES MORTAL BEAUTY

To what serves mortal beauty⎪– dangerous; does set danc-
ing blood – the O-seal-that-so⎪feature, flung prouder form
Than Purcell tune lets tread to?⎪See: it does this: keeps
    warm
Men's wits to the things that are;⎪what good means –
    where a glance
Master more may than gaze,⎪gaze out of countenance.
Those lovely lads once, wet-fresh⎪windfalls of war's storm,
How then should Gregory, a father,⎪have gleanèd else
    from swarm-
èd Rome? But God to a nation⎪dealt that day's dear chance.
To man, that needs would worship⎪block or barren stone,
Our law says: Love what are⎪love's worthiest, were all
    known;
World's loveliest – men's selves. Self⎪flashes off frame
    and face.
What do then? how meet beauty?⎪Merely meet it; own,
Home at heart, heaven's sweet gift;⎪then leave, let that
    alone.
Yea, wish that though, wish all,⎪God's better beauty,
    grace.

THAT NATURE IS A HERACLITEAN FIRE AND OF THE COMFORT OF THE RESURRECTION

Cloud-puffball, torn tufts, tossed pillows⎸flaunt forth,
    then chevy on an air-
built thoroughfare: heaven-roysterers, in gay-gangs⎸
    they throng; they glitter in marches.
Down roughcast, down dazzling whitewash,⎸wherever
    an elm arches,
Shivelights and shadowtackle in long⎸lashes lace,
    lance, and pair.
Delightfully the bright wind boisterous⎸ropes,
    wrestles, beats earth bare
Of yestertempest's creases;⎸in pool and rutpeel parches
Squandering ooze to squeezed⎸dough, crust, dust;
    stanches, starches
Squadroned masks and manmarks⎸treadmire toil there
Footfretted in it. Million-fuelèd,⎸nature's bonfire
    burns on.
But quench her bonniest, dearest⎸to her, her clearest-
    selvèd spark
Man, how fast his firedint,⎸his mark on mind, is gone!
Both are in an unfathomable, all is in an enormous dark
Drowned. O pity and indig⎸nation! Manshape, that
    shone
Sheer off, disseveral, a star,⎸death blots black out; nor mark

                 Is any of him at all so stark
But vastness blurs and time│beats level. Enough! the
      Resurrection,
A heart's-clarion! Away grief's gasping,│joyless
      days, dejection.
                     Across my foundering deck shone
A beacon, an eternal beam.│Flesh fade, and mortal trash
Fall to the residuary worm;│world's wildfire, leave but ash:
             In a flash, at a trumpet crash,
I am all at once what Christ is,│since he was what I am, and
This Jack, joke, poor potsherd,│patch, matchwood,
      immortal diamond,
                     Is immortal diamond.

MORNING, MIDDAY, AND EVENING SACRIFICE

The dappled die-away
Cheek and the wimpled lip,
The gold-wisp, the airy-grey
Eye, all in fellowship –
This, all this beauty blooming,
This, all this freshness fuming,
Give God while worth consuming.

Both thought and thew now bolder
And told by Nature: Tower;
Head, heart, hand, heel, and shoulder
That beat and breathe in power –
This pride of prime's enjoyment
Take as for tool not toy meant
And hold at Christ's employment.

The vault and scope and schooling
And mastery in the mind,
In silk-ash kept from cooling,
And ripest under rind –
What death half lifts the latch of,
What hell hopes soon the snatch of,
Your offering, with despatch, of!

THE SILVER JUBILEE:
To James First Bishop of Shrewsbury on the
25th Year of his Episcopate July 28, 1876.

Though no high-hung bells or din
Of braggart bugles cry it in –
    What is sound? Nature's round
Makes the Silver Jubilee.

Five and twenty years have run
Since sacred fountains to the sun
    Sprang, that but now were shut,
Showering Silver Jubilee.

Feasts, when we shall fall asleep,
Shrewsbury may see others keep;
    None but you this her true,
This her Silver Jubilee.

Not today we need lament
Your wealth of life is some way spent:
    Toil has shed round your head
Silver but for Jubilee.

Then for her whose velvet vales
Should have pealed with welcome, Wales,
    Let the chime of a rhyme
Utter Silver Jubilee.

THE LOSS OF THE EURYDICE
Foundered March 24, 1878

The Eurydice – it concerned thee, O Lord:
Three hundred souls, O alas! on board,
    Some asleep unawakened, all un-
warned, eleven fathoms fallen

Where she foundered! One stroke
Felled and furled them, the hearts of oak!
    And flockbells off the aerial
Downs' forefalls beat to the burial.

For did she pride her, freighted fully, on
Bounden bales or a hoard of bullion? –
    Precious passing measure,
Lads and men her lade and treasure.

She had come from a cruise, training seamen –
Men, boldboys soon to be men:
    Must it, worst weather,
Blast bole and bloom together?

No Atlantic squall overwrought her
Or rearing billow of the Biscay water:
    Home was hard at hand
And the blow bore from land.

And you were a liar, O blue March day.
Bright sun lanced fire in the heavenly bay;
    But what black Boreas wrecked her? he
Came equipped, deadly-electric,

A beetling baldbright cloud thorough England
Riding: there did storms not mingle? and
    Hailropes hustle and grind their
Heavengravel? wolfsnow, worlds of it, wind there?

Now Carisbrook keep goes under in gloom;
Now it overvaults Appledurcombe;
    Now near by Ventnor town
It hurls, hurls off Boniface Down.

Too proud, too proud, what a press she bore!
Royal, and all her royals wore.
    Sharp with her, shorten sail!
Too late; lost; gone with the gale.

This was that fell capsize.
As half she had righted and hoped to rise
    Death teeming in by her portholes
Raced down decks, round messes of mortals.

Then a lurch forward, frigate and men;
'All hands for themselves' the cry ran then;
       But she who had housed them thither
Was around them, bound them or wound them with her.

Marcus Hare, high her captain,
Kept to her – care-drowned and wrapped in
       Cheer's death, would follow
His charge through the champ-white
       water-in-a-wallow,

All under Channel to bury in a beach her
Cheeks: Right, rude of feature,
       He thought he heard say
'Her commander! and thou too, and thou this way.'

It is even seen, time's something server,
In mankind's medley a duty-swerver,
       At downright 'No or Yes?'
Doffs all, drives full for righteousness.

Sydney Fletcher, Bristol-bred,
(Low lie his mates now on watery bed)
       Takes to the seas and snows
As sheer down the ship goes.

Now her afterdraught gullies him too down;
Now he wrings for breath with the deathgush brown;
    Till a lifebelt and God's will
Lend him a lift from the sea-swill.

Now he shoots short up to the round air;
Now he gasps, now he gazes everywhere;
    But his eye no cliff, no coast or
Mark makes in the rivelling snowstorm.

Him, after an hour of wintry waves,
A schooner sights, with another, and saves,
    And he boards her in Oh! such joy
He has lost count what came next, poor boy. –

They say who saw one sea-corpse cold
He was all of lovely manly mould,
    Every inch a tar,
Of the best we boast our sailors are.

Look, foot to forelock, how all things suit! he
Is strung by duty, is strained to beauty,
    And brown-as-dawning-skinned
With brine and shine and whirling wind.

O his nimble finger, his gnarled grip!
Leagues, leagues of seamanship
    Slumber in these forsaken
Bones, this sinew, and will not waken.

He was but one like thousands more.
Day and night I deplore
    My people and born own nation,
Fast foundering own generation.

I might let bygones be – our curse
Of ruinous shrine no hand or, worse,
    Robbery's hand is busy to
Dress, hoar-hallowèd shrines unvisited;

Only the breathing temple and fleet
Life, this wildworth blown so sweet,
    These daredeaths, ay this crew, in
Unchrist, all rolled in ruin –

Deeply surely I need to deplore it,
Wondering why my master bore it,
    The riving off that race
So at home, time was, to his truth and grace

That a starlight-wender of ours would say
The marvellous Milk was Walsingham Way
    And one – but let be, let be:
More, more than was will yet be. –

O well wept, mother have lost son;
Wept, wife; wept, sweetheart would be one:
    Though grief yield them no good
Yet shed what tears sad truelove should.

But to Christ lord of thunder
Crouch; lay knee by earth low under:
    'Holiest, loveliest, bravest,
Save my hero, O Hero savest.

And the prayer thou hearst me making
Have, at the awful overtaking,
    Heard; have heard and granted
Grace that day grace was wanted.'

Not that hell knows redeeming,
But for souls sunk in seeming
    Fresh, till doomfire burn all,
Prayer shall fetch pity eternal.

THE WRECK OF THE DEUTSCHLAND

*To the happy memory of the five Franciscan nuns
exiles by the Falck Laws drowned between midnight
and morning of Dec. 7th, 1875*

PART THE FIRST

1

Thou mastering me
God! giver of breath and bread;
World's strand, sway of the sea;
Lord of living and dead;
Thou hast bound bones and veins in me, fastened
me flesh,
And after it almost unmade, what with dread,
Thy doing: and dost thou touch me afresh?
Over again I feel thy finger and find thee.

2

     I did say yes
    O at lightning and lashed rod;
  Thou heardst me truer than tongue confess
    Thy terror, O Christ, O God;
Thou knowest the walls, altar and hour and night:
  The swoon of a heart that the sweep and the hurl
    of thee trod
  Hard down with a horror of height:
And the midriff astrain with leaning of, laced with fire
    of stress.

3

    The frown of his face
  Before me, the hurtle of hell
Behind, where, where was a, where was a place?
    I whirled out wings that spell
And fled with a fling of the heart to the heart of the
    Host.
My heart, but you were dovewinged, I can tell,
  Carrier-witted, I am bold to boast,
To flash from the flame to the flame then, tower from
    the grace to the grace.

4

I am soft sift
In an hourglass – at the wall
Fast, but mined with a motion, a drift,
    And it crowds and it combs to the fall;
I steady as a water in a well, to a poise, to a pane,
But roped with, always, all the way down from the tall
    Fells or flanks of the voel, a vein
Of the gospel proffer, a pressure, a principle, Christ's gift.

5

I kiss my hand
To the stars, lovely-asunder
Starlight, wafting him out of it; and
    Glow, glory in thunder;
Kiss my hand to the dappled-with-damson west:
Since, tho' he is under the world's splendour and
    wonder,
    His mystery must be instressed, stressed;
For I greet him the days I meet him, and bless when I
    understand.

6

Not out of his bliss
Springs the stress felt
Nor first from heaven (and few know this)
Swings the stroke dealt —
Stroke and a stress that stars and storms deliver,
That guilt is hushed by, hearts are flushed by and
melt —
But it rides time like riding a river
(And here the faithful waver, the faithless fable and miss).

7

It dates from day
Of his going in Galilee;
Warm-laid grave of a womb-life grey;
Manger, maiden's knee;
The dense and the driven Passion, and frightful
sweat:
Thence the discharge of it, there its swelling to be,
Though felt before, though in high flood yet —
What none would have known of it, only the heart, being
hard at bay,

8

Is out with it! Oh,
We lash with the best or worst
Word last! How a lush-kept plush-capped sloe
Will, mouthed to flesh-burst,
Gush! – flush the man, the being with it, sour or
sweet,
Brim, in a flash, full! – Hither then, last or first,
To hero of Calvary, Christ's feet –
Never ask if meaning it, wanting it, warned of it – men go.

9

Be adored among men,
God, three-numberèd form;
Wring thy rebel, dogged in den,
Man's malice, with wrecking and storm.
Beyond saying sweet, past telling of tongue,
Thou art lightning and love, I found it, a winter
and warm;
Father and fondler of heart thou hast wrung:
Hast thy dark descending and most art merciful then.

10

With an anvil-ding
And with fire in him forge thy will
Or rather, rather then, stealing as Spring
Through him, melt him but master him still:
Whether at once, as once at a crash Paul,
Or as Austin, a lingering-out swéet skíll,
Make mercy in all of us, out of us all
Mastery, but be adored, but be adored King.

PART THE SECOND

11

'Some find me a sword; some
The flange and the rail; flame,
Fang, or flood' goes Death on drum,
And storms bugle his fame.
But wé dream we are rooted in earth – Dust!
Flesh falls within sight of us, we, though our
flower the same,
Wave with the meadow, forget that there must
The sour scythe cringe, and the blear share come.

12

On Saturday sailed from Bremen,
American-outward-bound,
Take settler and seamen, tell men with women,
Two hundred souls in the round –
O Father, not under thy feathers nor ever as
guessing
The goal was a shoal, of a fourth the doom to be
drowned;
Yet did the dark side of the bay of thy blessing
Not vault them, the million of rounds of thy mercy not
reeve even them in?

13

Into the snows she sweeps,
Hurling the haven behind,
The Deutschland, on Sunday; and so the sky
keeps,
For the infinite air is unkind,
And the sea flint-flake, black-backed in the regular
blow,
Sitting Eastnortheast, in cursed quarter, the wind;
Wiry and white-fiery and whirlwind-
swivellèd snow
Spins to the widow-making unchilding unfathering deeps.

14

She drove in the dark to leeward,
She struck – not a reef or a rock
But the combs of a smother of sand: night
drew her
Dead to the Kentish Knock;
And she beat the bank down with her bows and the
ride of her keel:
The breakers rolled on her beam with ruinous shock;
And canvas and compass, the whorl and the
wheel
Idle for ever to waft her or wind her with, these she
endured.

15

Hope had grown grey hairs,
Hope had mourning on,
Trenched with tears, carved with cares,
Hope was twelve hours gone;
And frightful a nightfall folded rueful a day
Nor rescue, only rocket and lightship, shone,
And lives at last were washing away:
To the shrouds they took, – they shook in the hurling
and horrible airs.

16

One stirred from the rigging to save
The wild woman-kind below,
With a rope's end round the man, handy and brave —
He was pitched to his death at a blow,
For all his dreadnought breast and braids of thew:
They could tell him for hours, dandled the to and fro
Through the cobbled foam-fleece. What could
he do
With the burl of the fountains of air, buck and the flood
of the wave?

17

They fought with God's cold —
And they could not and fell to the deck
(Crushed them) or water (and drowned them)
or rolled
With the sea-romp over the wreck.
Night roared, with the heart-break hearing a heart-
broke rabble,
The woman's wailing, the crying of child without
check —
Till a lioness arose breasting the babble,
A prophetess towered in the tumult, a virginal tongue told.

18

Ah, touched in your bower of bone,
Are you! turned for an exquisite smart,
Have you! make words break from me here all
alone,
Do you! – mother of being in me, heart.
O unteachably after evil, but uttering truth,
Why, tears! is it? tears; such a melting, a madrigal
start!
Never-eldering revel and river of youth,
What can it be, this glee? the good you have there of
your own?

19

Sister, a sister calling
A master, her master and mine! –
And the inboard seas run swirling and
hawling;
The rash smart sloggering brine
Blinds her; but she that weather sees one thing, one;
Has one fetch in her; she rears herself to divine
Ears, and the call of the tall nun
To the men in the tops and the tackle rode over the
storm's brawling.

20

She was first of a five and came
        Of a coifèd sisterhood.
(O Deutschland, double a desperate name!
        O world wide of its good!
But Gertrude, lily, and Luther, are two of a town,
    Christ's lily and beast of the waste wood:
        From life's dawn it is drawn down,
Abel is Cain's brother and breasts they have sucked the
    same.)

21

Loathed for a love men knew in them,
        Banned by the land of their birth,
    Rhine refused them, Thames would ruin them;
        Surf, snow, river and earth
Gnashed: but thou art above, thou Orion of light;
    Thy unchancelling poising palms were weighing the
        worth,
        Thou martyr-master: in thy sight
Storm flakes were scroll-leaved flowers, lily showers –
    sweet heaven was astrew in them.

22

Five! the finding and sake
And cipher of suffering Christ.
Mark, the mark is of man's make
And the word of it Sacrificed.
But he scores it in scarlet himself on his own
bespoken,
Before-time-taken, dearest prizèd and priced –
Stigma, signal, cinquefoil token
For lettering of the lamb's fleece, ruddying of the
rose-flake.

Joy fall to thee, father Francis,
Drawn to the Life that died;
With the gnarls of the nails in thee, niche of
the lance, his
Lovescape crucified
And seal of his seraph-arrival! and these thy
daughters
And five-livèd and leavèd favour and pride,
Are sisterly sealed in wild waters,
To bathe in his fall-gold mercies, to breathe in his all-
fire glances.

24

Away in the loveable west,
On a pastoral forehead of Wales,
I was under a roof here, I was at rest,
And they the prey of the gales;
She to the black-about air, to the breaker, the
thickly
Falling flakes, to the throng that catches and quails
Was calling 'O Christ, Christ, come quickly':
The cross to her she calls Christ to her, christens her
wild-worst Best.

25

The majesty! what did she mean?
Breathe, arch and original Breath.
Is it love in her of the being as her lover had
been?
Breathe, body of lovely Death.
They were else-minded then, altogether, the men
Woke thee with a *We are perishing* in the weather
of Genesareth.
Or is it that she cried for the crown then,
The keener to come at the comfort for feeling the
combating keen?

26

     For how to the heart's cheering
       The down-dugged ground-hugged grey
Hovers off, the jay-blue heavens appearing
       Of pied and peeled May!
Blue-beating and hoary-glow height; or night,
      still higher,
With belled fire and the moth-soft Milky Way,
     What by your measure is the heaven of desire,
The treasure never eyesight got, nor was ever guessed
    what for the hearing?

27

     No, but it was not these.
     The jading and jar of the cart,
    Time's tasking, it is fathers that asking for
      ease
     Of the sodden-with-its-sorrowing heart,
Not danger, electrical horror; then further it finds
The appealing of the Passion is tenderer in prayer
     apart:
     Other, I gather, in measure her mind's
Burden, in wind's burly and beat of endragonèd seas.

28

But how shall I . . . make me room there:
Reach me a . . . Fancy, come faster –
Strike you the sight of it? look at it loom
    there,
    Thing that she . . . There then! the Master,
Ipse, the only one, Christ, King, Head:
He was to cure the extremity where he had cast her;
    Do, deal, lord it with living and dead;
Let him ride, her pride, in his triumph, despatch and
    have done with his doom there.

29

Ah! there was a heart right!
There was single eye!
Read the unshapeable shock night
    And knew the who and the why;
Wording it how but by him that present and past,
    Heaven and earth are word of, worded by? –
    The Simon Peter of a soul! to the blast
Tarpeïan-fast, but a blown beacon of light.

30

Jesu, heart's light,
Jesu, maid's son,
What was the feast followed the night
Thou hadst glory of this nun? —
Feast of the one woman without stain.
For so conceivèd, so to conceive thee is done;
But here was heart-throe, birth of a brain,
Word, that heard and kept thee and uttered thee
outright.

31

Well, she has thee for the pain, for the
Patience; but pity of the rest of them!
Heart, go and bleed at a bitterer vein for the
Comfortless unconfessed of them —
No not uncomforted: lovely-felicitous Providence
Finger of a tender of, O of a feathery delicacy, the
breast of the
Maiden could obey so, be a bell to, ring of it, and
Startle the poor sheep back! is the shipwrack then a
harvest, does tempest carry the grain for thee?

32

I admire thee, master of the tides,
　　Of the Yore-flood, of the year's fall;
The recurb and the recovery of the gulf's sides,
　　　The girth of it and the wharf of it and the
　　　　wall;
Stanching, quenching ocean of a motionable mind;
Ground of being, and granite of it: past all
　　Grasp God, throned behind
Death with a sovereignty that heeds but hides, bodes but
　abides;

33

　　With a mercy that outrides
　　The all of water, an ark
For the listener; for the lingerer with a love
　　glides
　　Lower than death and the dark;
A vein for the visiting of the past-prayer, pent in
　prison,
The-last-breath penitent spirits – the uttermost
　mark
　　Our passion-plungèd giant risen,
The Christ of the Father compassionate, fetched in the
　storm of his strides.

34

Now burn, new born to the world,
Double-naturèd name,
The heaven-flung, heart-fleshed,
maiden-furled
Miracle-in-Mary-of-flame,
Mid-numberèd he in three of the thunder-throne!
Not a dooms-day dazzle in his coming nor dark as
he came;
Kind, but royally reclaiming his own;
A released shower, let flash to the shire, not a lightning
of fire hard-hurled.

Dame, at our door
Drowned, and among our shoals,
Remember us in the roads, the heaven-haven
of the reward:
Our King back, Oh, upon English souls!
Let him easter in us, be a dayspring to the dimness
of us, be a crimson-cresseted east,
More brightening her, rare-dear Britain, as his
reign rolls,
Pride, rose, prince, hero of us, high-priest,
Our hearts' charity's hearth's fire, our thoughts'
chivalry's throng's Lord.

SELECTED PROSE

AUTHOR'S PREFACE

The poems in this book are written some in Running Rhythm, the common rhythm in English use, some in Sprung Rhythm, and some in a mixture of the two. And those in the common rhythm are some counterpointed, some not.

Common English rhythm, called Running Rhythm above, is measured by feet of either two or three syllables and (putting aside the imperfect feet at the beginning and end of lines and also some unusual measures in which feet seem to be paired together and double or composite feet to arise) never more nor less.

Every foot has one principal stress or accent, and this or the syllable it falls on may be called the Stress of the foot and the other part, the one or two unaccented syllables, the Slack. Feet (and the rhythms made out of them) in which the Stress comes first are called Falling Feet and Falling Rhythms, feet and rhythm in which the Slack comes first are called Rising Feet and Rhythms, and if the Stress is between two Slacks there will be Rocking Feet and Rhythms. These distinctions are real and true to nature; but for purposes of scanning it is a great convenience to follow the example of music and take the stress always first, as the accent or the chief accent always comes first in a musical bar. If this is done there will be in common English verse only two possible feet – the so-called accentual Trochee and Dactyl, and correspondingly only two possible uniform rhythms, the so-called Trochaic and Dactylic. But they may be mixed and then what the Greeks called a Logaoedic Rhythm arises. These are the facts and according to these the scanning of ordinary regularly-written English verse is very simple indeed and to bring in other principles is here unnecessary.

But because verse written strictly in these feet and by these principles will become same and tame the poets have brought in licences and departures from rule to give variety, and especially when the natural rhythm is rising, as in the common ten-syllable or five-foot verse, rhymed or blank. These irregularities are chiefly Reversed Feet and Reversed or Counterpoint Rhythm, which two things are two steps or degrees of licence in the same kind. By a reversed foot I mean the putting the stress where, to judge by the rest of the measure, the slack should be and the slack where the stress, and this is done freely at the beginning of a line and, in the course of a line, after a pause; only scarcely ever in the second foot or place and never in the last, unless when the poet designs some extraordinary effect; for these places are characteristic and sensitive and cannot well be touched. But the reversal of the first foot and of some middle foot after a strong pause is a thing so natural that our poets have generally done it, from Chaucer down, without remark and it commonly passes un-noticed and cannot be said to amount to a formal change of rhythm, but rather is that irregularity which all natural growth and motion shews. If however the reversal is repeated in two feet running, especially so as to include the sensitive second foot, it must be due either to great want of ear or else is a calculated effect, the superinducing or *mounting* of a new rhythm upon the old; and since the new or mounted rhythm is actually heard and at the same time the mind naturally supplies the natural or standard foregoing rhythm, for we do not forget what the rhythm is that by rights we should be hearing, two rhythms are in some manner running at once and we have something answerable to counter-point in music, which is two or more strains of tune going on together, and this is Counterpoint Rhythm. Of this kind of verse Milton is the great master and the choruses of *Samson Agonistes* are written throughout in it – but with the disadvantage that he does not let the reader clearly know what the ground-rhythm is meant to be and so they have struck most readers as merely irregular. And in fact if you counterpoint throughout, since one only of the counter rhythms is actually heard, the other is really destroyed or cannot come to exist and what is written is one rhythm only and probably Sprung Rhythm, of which I now speak.

Sprung Rhythm, as used in this book, is measured by

feet of from one to four syllables, regularly, and for particular effects any number of weak or slack syllables may be used. It has one stress, which falls on the only syllable, if there is only one, or if there are more, then scanning as above, on the first, and so gives rise to four sorts of feet, a monosyllable and the so-called accentual Trochee, Dactyl, and the First Paeon. And there will be four corresponding natural rhythms; but nominally the feet are mixed and any one may follow any other. And hence Sprung Rhythm differs from Running Rhythm in having or being only one nominal rhythm, a mixed or 'logaoedic' one, instead of three, but on the other hand in having twice the flexibility of foot, so that any two stresses may either follow one another running or be divided by one, two, or three slack syllables. But strict Sprung Rhythm cannot be counterpointed. In Sprung Rhythm, as in logaoedic rhythm generally, the feet are assumed to be equally long or strong and their seeming inequality is made up by pause or stressing.

Remark also that it is natural in Sprung Rhythm for the lines to be *rove over*, that is for the scanning of each line immediately to take up that of the one before, so that if the first has one or more syllables at its end the other must have so many the less at its beginning; and in fact the scanning runs on without break from the beginning, say, of a stanza to the end and all the stanza is one long strain, though written in lines asunder.

Two licences are natural to Sprung Rhythm. The one is rests, as in music; but of this an example is scarcely to be found in this book, unless in the *Echos*, second line. The other is *hangers* or *outrides*, that is one, two, or three slack syllables added to a foot and not counting in the nominal scanning. They are so called because they seem to hang below the line or ride forward or backward from it in another dimension than the line itself, according to a principle needless to explain here. These outriding half feet or hangers are marked by a loop underneath them, and plenty of them will be found.

The other marks are easily understood, namely accents, where the reader might be in doubt which syllable should have the stress; slurs, that is loops *over* syllables, to tie them together into the time of one; little loops at the end of a line to shew that the rhyme goes on to the first letter of the next line; what in music are called pauses ⌢, to shew that the syllable should be dwelt on; and twirls ∞, to mark reversed or counter-pointed rhythm.

Note on the nature and history of Sprung Rhythm – Sprung Rhythm is the most natural of things. For (1) it is the rhythm of common speech and of written prose, when rhythm is perceived in them. (2) It is the rhythm of all but the most monotonously regular music, so that in the words of choruses and refrains and in songs written closely to music it arises. (3) It is found in nursery rhymes, weather saws, and so on; because, however these may have been once made in running rhythm, the terminations having dropped off by the change of language, the stresses come together and so the rhythm is sprung. (4) It arises in common verse when reversed or counterpointed, for the same reason.

But nevertheless in spite of all this and though Greek and Latin lyric verse, which is well known, and the old English verse seen in *Pierce Ploughman* are in sprung rhythm, it has in fact ceased to be used since the Elizabethan age, Greene being the last writer who can be said to have recognized it. For perhaps there was not, down to our days, a single, even short, poem in English in which sprung rhythm is employed – not for single effects or in fixed places – but as the governing principle of the scansion. I say this because the contrary has been asserted: if it is otherwise the poem should be cited.

POETRY AND VERSE

Is all verse poetry or all poetry verse? – Depends on definitions of both. Poetry is speech framed for contemplation of the mind by the way of hearing or speech framed to be heard for its own sake and interest even over and above its interest of meaning. Some matter and meaning is essential to it but only as an element necessary to support and employ the shape which is contemplated for its own sake. (Poetry is in fact speech only employed to carry the inscape of speech for the inscape's sake – and therefore the inscape must be dwelt on. Now if this can be done without repeating it *once* of the inscape will be enough for art and beauty and poetry but then at least the inscape must be understood as so standing by itself that it could be copied and repeated. If not/ repetition, *oftening, over-and-overing, aftering* of the inscape must take place in order to detach it to the mind and in this light poetry is speech which afters and oftens its inscape, speech couched in a repeating figure and verse is spoken sound having a repeating figure.) Verse is (inscape of spoken sound, not spoken words, or speech employed to carry the inscape of spoken sound – or in the usual words) speech wholly or partially repeating the same figure of sound. Now there is speech which wholly or partially repeats the same figure of grammar and this may be framed to be heard for its own sake and interest over and above its interest of meaning. Poetry then may be couched in this, and therefore all poetry is not verse but all poetry is either verse or falls under this or some still further development of what verse is, speech wholly or partially repeating some kind of figure which is over and above meaning, at least the grammatical, historical, and logical meaning.

But is all verse poetry? – Verse may be applied for use, e.g. to help the memory, and then is useful art, not μουσική ('Thirty days hath September' and 'Propria quae maribus' or Livy's *horrendum carmen*) and so is not poetry. Or it might be composed without meaning (as nonsense verse and choruses – 'Hey nonny nonny' or 'Wille wau wau wau' etc) and then *alone* it would not be poetry but might be part of a poem. But if it has a meaning and is meant to be heard for its own sake it will be poetry if you take poetry to be a kind of composition and not the virtue or success or excellence of that kind, as eloquence is the virtue of oratory and not oratory only and beauty the virtue of inscape and not inscape only. In this way poetry may be high or low, good or bad, and doggrel will be poor or low poetry but not merely verse, for it aims at interest or amusement. But if poetry is the virtue of its own kind of composition then all verse even composed for its own interest's sake is not poetry.

Kinds of Verse—

Verse then is speech wholly or partially repeating the same figure of sound. Partially as 'Jam satis terris nivis atque dirae' – that is $/-\cup--|-\cup\cup-|\cup--$, for the common measure $\cup$ ($=\frac{1}{2}-$) is repeated throughout, wholly when you add 'Grandinis misit Pater et rubente'; or partially, taking the whole stanza, for it repeats the same figure for three lines but gives up in the fourth, but wholly if you take two stanzas. More clearly such an iambic as this $-\cup\cup\stackrel{\prime}{-}|\cup\stackrel{\prime}{-}$ $|-\acute{\cup}\cup|\cup\acute{\cup}\cup|-\stackrel{\prime}{-}|\cup\acute{\cup}-$ is a partial repetition only, for this is verse though you did not add another line, and this is a whole repetition $-\cup\stackrel{\prime}{-}|\cup\stackrel{\prime}{-}|\cup\stackrel{\prime}{-}$ $|\cup\stackrel{\prime}{-}|\cup\stackrel{\prime}{-}|\cup\stackrel{\prime}{-}$.

It is speech because we must distinguish it from music which is not verse. Music is composition which wholly or partially repeats the same figure of pitched sound (it is the aftering of pitched sound). Verse must be spoken or capable of being spoken.

The figure may be repeated runningly, continuously, as in rhythm (ABABAB) or intermittently, as in alliteration and rhyme (ABCDABEFABGH). The former gives more tone, *candorem*, style, chasteness; the latter more brilliancy, starriness, quain, margaretting.

[There are three artistic tones – *candor*, chasteness, 'clear', which is diffused beauty; humour, which is diffused wit; and pathos, which is diffused.]

FROM THE LETTERS

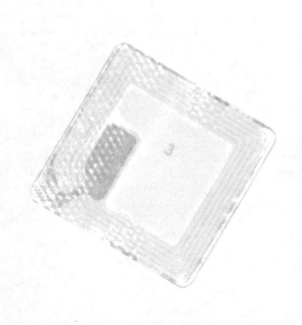

To A. W. M. Baillie   10 September 1864

... Do you know, a horrible thing has happened to me. I have begun to *doubt* Tennyson. (Baillejus ap. Hopk.) It is a great *argumentum*, a great clue, that our minds jump together even if it be a leap into the dark. I cannot tell you how amused and I must say pleased and comforted by this coincidence I am. A little explanation first. You know I do not mistrust my judgment so soon as you do; I say it to the praise of your modesty. Therefore I do not think myself 'getting into my dotage' for that, and I will shew why. I think (I am assuming a great deal in saying this I fear) I may shew, judging from my own mind, how far we are both of us right in this, and on what, if I may use the word, more *enlightened* ground we may set our admiration of Tennyson. I have been thinking about this on and off since I read *Enoch Arden* and the other new poems, so that my judgment is more digested than if the ideas had only struck me while answering you. I was shaken too you know by Addis, which makes a good deal of difference.

I am meditating an essay, perhaps for the *Hexameron*, on some points of poetical criticism, and it is with reference to this a little that I have composed my thoughts on Tennyson. I think then the language of verse may be divided into three kinds. The first and highest is poetry proper, the language of inspiration.

The word inspiration need cause no difficulty. I mean by it a mood of great, abnormal in fact, mental acuteness, either energetic or receptive, according as the thoughts which arise in it seem generated by a stress and action of the brain, or to strike into it unasked. This mood arises from various causes, physical generally, as good health or state of the air or, prosaic as it is, length of time after a meal. But I need not go into this; all that it is needful to mark is, that the poetry of inspiration can only be written in this mood of mind, even if it only last a minute, by poets themselves. Everybody of course has like moods, but not being poets what they then produce is not poetry. The second kind I call *Parnassian*. It can only be spoken by poets, but is not in the highest sense poetry. It does not require the mood of mind in which the poetry of inspiration is written. It is spoken *on and from the level* of a poet's mind, not, as in the other case, when the inspiration which is the gift of genius, raises him above himself. For I think it is the case with genius that it is not when quiescent so very much above mediocrity as the difference between the two might lead us to think, but that it has the power and privilege of rising from that level to a height utterly far from mediocrity: in other words that its greatness is *that it can be* so great. You will understand. *Parnassian* then is that language which genius speaks as fitted to its exaltation, and place among other genius, but does not sing (I have been betrayed into the whole hog of a metaphor) in its flights. Great men, poets I mean, have each their own dialect as it were of Parnassian, formed generally as they go on writing, and at last, – this is the point to be marked, – they can see things in this Parnassian way and describe them in this Parnassian tongue, without further effort of inspiration. In a poet's particular kind of Parnassian lies most of his style, of his manner, of his mannerism if you like. But I must not go farther without giving you instances of Parnassian. I shall take one from Tennyson, and from *Enoch Arden*, from a passage much quoted already and which will be no doubt often quoted, the description of Enoch's tropical island.

> The mountain wooded to the peak, the lawns
> And winding glades high up like ways to Heaven,
> The slender coco's drooping crown of plumes,
> The lightning flash of insect and of bird,
> The lustre of the long convolvuluses
> That coil'd around the stately stems, and ran
> Ev'n to the limit of the land, the glows
> And glories of the broad belt of the world,
> All these he saw.

Now it is a mark of Parnassian that one could conceive oneself writing it if one were the poet. Do not say that *if* you were Shakespear you can imagine yourself writing Hamlet, because that is just what I think you can*not* conceive. In a fine piece of inspiration every beauty takes you as it were by surprise, not of course that you did not think the writer could be so great, for that is not it, – indeed I think it is a mistake to speak of people admiring Shakespear more and more as they live, for when the judgment is ripe and you have read a good deal of any writer including his best things, and carefully, then, I think, however high the place you give him, that you must have rated him equally with his merits however great they be; so that all after admiration cannot increase but keep alive this estimate, make his greatness stare into your eyes and din it into your ears, as it were, but not make it greater, – but to go on with the broken sentence, every fresh beauty could not in any way be predicted or accounted for by what one has already read. But in Parnassian pieces you feel that if you were the poet you could have gone on as he has done, you see yourself doing it, only with the difference that if you actually try you find you cannot write his Parnassian. Well now to turn to the piece above. The glades being 'like ways to Heaven' is, I think, a new thought, it is an inspiration. Not so the next line, that is pure Parnassian. If you examine it the words are choice and the description is beautiful and unexceptionable, but it does not *touch* you. The next is more Parnassian still. In the next lines I think the picture of the convolvuluses does touch; but only the

132

picture: the words are Parnassian. It is a very good instance, for the lines are undoubtedly beautiful, but yet I could scarcely point anywhere to anything more idiomatically Parnassian, to anything which I more clearly see myself writing *qua* Tennyson, than the words

The glows
And glories of the broad belt of the world.

What Parnassian is you will now understand, but I must make some more remarks on it. I believe that when a poet palls on us it is because of his Parnassian. We seem to have found out his secret. Now in fact we have not found out more than this, that when he is not inspired and in his flights, his poetry does run in an intelligibly laid down path. Well, it is notorious that Shakespear does not pall, and this is because he uses, I believe, so little Parnassian. He does use some, but little. Now judging from my own experience I should say no author palls so much as Wordsworth; this is because he writes such an 'intolerable deal of' Parnassian.

If with a critical eye and in a critical appreciative mood you read a poem by an unknown author or an anonymous poem by a known, but not at once recognizable, author, and he is a real poet, then you will pronounce him so at once, and the poem will seem truly inspired, though afterwards, when you know the author, you will be able to distinguish his inspirations from his Parnassian, and will perhaps think the very piece which struck you so much at first mere Parnassian. You know well how deadened, as it were, the critical faculties become at times, when all good poetry alike loses its clear ring and its charm; while in other moods they are so enlivened that things that have long lost their freshness strike you with their original definiteness and piquant beauty.

I think one had got into the way of thinking, or had not got out of the way of thinking, that Tennyson was always new, *touching*, beyond other poets, not pressed with human ailments, never using Parnassian. So at least I used to think. Now one sees he uses Parnassian; he is, one must see it, what we used to call Tennysonian. But the discovery of this must not make too much difference. When puzzled by one's doubts it is well to turn to a passage like this. Surely your maturest judgment will never be fooled out of saying that this is divine, terribly beautiful – the stanza of *In Memoriam* beginning with the quatrain

> O Hesper o'er the buried sun,
> And ready thou to die with him,
> Thou watchest all things ever dim
> And dimmer, and a glory done.

I quote from memory. Inconsequent conclusion: Shakespear is and must be utterly the greatest of poets.

Just to end what I was saying about poetry. There is a higher sort of Parnassian which I call *Castalian*, or it may be thought the lowest kind of inspiration. Beautiful poems may be written wholly in it. Its peculiarity is that though you can hardly conceive yourself having written in it, if in the poet's place, yet it is too characteristic of the poet, too so-and-so-all-over-ish, to be quite inspiration. E.g.

> Yet despair
> Touches me not, though pensive as a bird
> Whose vernal coverts winter hath laid bare.

This is from Wordsworth, beautiful, but rather too essentially Wordsworthian, too persistently his way of looking at things. The third kind is merely the language of verse as distinct from that of prose, Delphic, the tongue of the Sacred *Plain*, I may call it, used in common by poet and poetaster. Poetry when spoken is spoken in it, but to speak it is not necessarily to speak poetry. I may add there is also *Olympian*. This is the language of strange masculine genius which suddenly, as it were, forces its way into the domain of poetry, without naturally having a right there. Milman's poetry is of this kind I think, and Rossetti's *Blessèd Damozel*. But unusual poetry has a tendency to seem so at first ...

To Robert Bridges   21 August 1877

Dearest Bridges,

Your letter cannot amuse Father Provincial, for he is on the unfathering deeps outward bound to Jamaica: I shd. not think of telling you anything about his reverence's goings and comings if it were not that I know this fact has been chronicled in the Catholic papers.

Enough that it amuses me, especially the story about Wooldridge and the Wagnerite, wh. is very good.

Your parody reassures me about your understanding the metre. Only remark, as you say that there is no conceivable licence I shd. not be able to justify, that with all my licences, or rather laws, I am stricter than you and I might say than anybody I know. With the exception of the *Bremen* stanza, which was, I think, the first written after 10 years' interval of silence, and before I had fixed my principles, my rhymes are rigidly good – to the ear – and such rhymes as *love* and *prove* I scout utterly. And my quantity is not like 'Fīftўtwō Bĕdfŏrd Squāre', where *fīftў* might pass but *Bĕdfŏrd* I should never admit. Not only so but Swinburne's dactyls and anapaests are halting to my ear: I never allow e.g. *I* or *my* (that is diphthongs, for *I = a + i* and *my = ma + i*) in the short or weak syllables of those feet, excepting before vowels, semi-vowels, or *r*, and rarely then, or when the measure becomes (what is the word?)

136

molossic – thus: ∪ – ∪ | ∪ – ∪ | ∪ – ∪, for then the
first short is almost long. If you look again you will see.
So that I may say my apparent licences are counter-
balanced, and more, by my strictness. In fact all English
verse, except Milton's, almost, offends me as 'licen-
tious'. Remember this.

I do not of course claim to have invented *sprung
rhythms* but only *sprung rhythm*; I mean that single lines
and single instances of it are not uncommon in English
and I have pointed them out in lecturing – e.g. 'why
should this : desert be?' – which the editors have
variously amended; 'There to meet : with Macbeth' or
'There to meet with Mac : beth'; Campbell has some
throughout the *Battle of the Baltic* – 'and their fleet along
the deep : proudly shone' – and *Ye Mariners* – 'as ye
sweep : through the deep' etc; Moore has some which I
cannot recall; there is one in *Grongar Hill*; and, not to
speak of *Pom pom*, in Nursery Rhymes, Weather Saws,
and Refrains they are very common – but what I do in
the *Deutschland* etc is to enfranchise them as a regular
and permanent principle of scansion.

There are no outriding feet in the *Deutschland*. An
outriding foot is, by a sort of contradiction, a recog-
nized extra-metrical effect; it is and it is not part of the
metre; not part of it, not being counted, but part of it by
producing a calculated effect which tells in the general
success. But the long, e.g. seven-syllabled, feet of the

Deutschland, are strictly metrical. Outriding feet belong to counterpointed verse, which supposes a well-known and unmistakeable or unforgettable standard rhythm: the *Deutschland* is not counterpointed; counterpoint is excluded by sprung rhythm. But in some of my sonnets I have mingled the two systems: this is the most delicate and difficult business of all.

The choruses in *Samson Agonistes* are intermediate between counterpointed and sprung rhythm. In reality they are sprung, but Milton keeps up a fiction of counterpointing the heard rhythm (which is the same as the mounted rhythm) upon a standard rhythm which is never heard but only counted and therefore really does not exist. The want of a metrical notation and the fear of being thought to write mere rhythmic or (who knows what the critics might not have said?) even unrhythmic prose drove him to this. Such rhythm as French and Welsh poetry has is sprung, counterpointed upon a counted rhythm, but it differs from Milton's in being little calculated, not more perhaps than prose consciously written rhythmically, like orations for instance; it is in fact the *native rhythm* of the words used bodily imported into verse; whereas Milton's mounted rhythm is a real poetical rhythm, having its own laws and recurrence, but further embarrassed by having to count.

Why do I employ sprung rhythm at all? Because it is

the nearest to the rhythm of prose, that is the native and natural rhythm of speech, the least forced, the most rhetorical and emphatic of all possible rhythms, combining, as it seems to me, opposite and, one wd. have thought, incompatible excellences, markedness of rhythm – that is rhythm's self – and naturalness of expression – for why, if it is forcible in prose to say 'lashed : rod', am I obliged to weaken this in verse, which ought to be stronger, not weaker, into 'láshed birch-ród' or something?

My verse is less to be read than heard, as I have told you before; it is oratorical, that is the rhythm is so. I think if you will study what I have here said you will be much more pleased with it and may I say? converted to it.

You ask may you call it 'presumptious jugglery'. No, but only for this reason, that *presumptious* is not English.

I cannot think of altering anything. Why shd. I? I do not write for the public. You are my public and I hope to convert you.

You say you wd. not for any money read my poem again. Nevertheless I beg you will. Besides money, you know, there is love. If it is obscure do not bother yourself with the meaning but pay attention to the best and most intelligible stanzas, as the two last of each part and the narrative of the wreck. If you had done this you wd. have liked it better and sent me some serviceable criticisms, but now your criticism is of no use, being only a protest memorialising me against my whole policy and proceedings.

I may add for your greater interest and edification that what refers to myself in the poem is all strictly and literally true and did all occur; nothing is added for poetical padding.

Believe me your affectionate friend

Gerard M. Hopkins S.J.

To Robert Bridges   2 April 1878

... I enclose you my Eurydice, which the *Month* refused. It is my only copy. Write no bilgewater about it: I will presently tell you what that is and till then excuse the term. I must tell you I am sorry you never read the Deutschland again.

Granted that it needs study and is obscure, for indeed I was not over-desirous that the meaning of all should be quite clear, at least unmistakeable, you might, without the effort that to make it all out would seem to have required, have nevertheless read it so that lines and stanzas should be left in the memory and superficial impressions deepened, and have liked some without exhausting all. I am sure I have read and enjoyed pages of poetry that way. Why, sometimes one enjoys and admires the very lines one cannot understand, as for instance 'If it were done when 'tis done' sqq., which is all obscure and disputed, though how fine it is everybody sees and nobody disputes. And so of many more passages in Shakspere and others. Besides you would have got more weathered to the style and its features – not really odd. Now they say that vessels sailing from the port of London will take (perhaps it should be / used once to take) Thames water for the voyage: it was foul and stunk at first as the ship worked but by degrees casting its filth was in a few days very pure and sweet and wholesomer and better than any water in the world. However that maybe, it is true to my purpose. When a new thing, such as my ventures in the Deutschland are, is presented us our first criticisms are not our truest, best, most homefelt, or most lasting but what come easiest on the instant. They are barbarous and like what the ignorant and the ruck say. This was so with you. The Deutschland on her first run worked very much and unsettled you, thickening and clouding your mind with vulgar mudbottom and common sewage (I see that I am going it with the image) and just then unhappily you *drew off* your criticisms all stinking (a necessity now of the image) and bilgy, whereas if you had let your thoughts cast themselves they would have been clearer in themselves and more to my taste too. I did not heed them therefore, perceiving they were a first drawing-off. Same of the Eurydice – which being short and easy please read more than once ...

To R. W. Dixon   5 October 1878

... I quite agree with what you write about Milton. His verse as one reads it seems something necessary and eternal (so to me does Purcell's music). As for 'proper hue', *now* it wd. be priggish, but I suppose Milton means *own hue* and they talk of *proper colours* in heraldry; not but what there is a Puritan touch about the line even so. However the word must once have had a different feeling. The Welsh have borrowed it for *pretty*; they talk of birds singing 'properly' and a little Welsh boy to whom I shewed the flowers in a green house exclaimed 'They *are* proper!' – Milton seems now coming to be studied better, and Masson is writing or has written his life at prodigious length. There was an interesting review by Matthew Arnold in one of the Quarterlies of 'a French critic on Milton' – Scherer I think. The same M. Arnold says Milton and Campbell are our two greatest masters of *style*. Milton's art is incomparable, not only in English literature but, I shd. think, almost in any; equal, if not more than equal, to the finest of Greek or Roman. And considering that this is shewn especially in his verse, his rhythm and metrical system, it is amazing that so great a writer as Newman should have fallen into the blunder of comparing the first chorus of the *Agonistes* with the opening of *Thalaba* as instancing the gain in smoothness and correctness of versification made since Milton's time – Milton having been not only ahead of his own time as well as all aftertimes in verse-structure but these particular choruses being his own highwater mark. It is as if you were to compare the Panathenaic frieze and a teaboard and decide in the teaboard's favour.

I have paid a good deal of attention to Milton's versification and collected his later rhythms: I did it when I had to lecture on rhetoric some years since. I found his most advanced effects in the *Paradise Regained* and, lyrically, in the *Agonistes*. I have often thought of writing on them, indeed on rhythm in general; I think the subject is little understood.

You ask, do I write verse myself. What I had written I burnt before I became a Jesuit and resolved to write no more, as not belonging to my profession, unless it were by the wish of my superiors; so for seven years I wrote nothing but two or three little presentation pieces which occasion called for. But when in the winter of '75 the Deutschland was wrecked in the mouth of the Thames and five Franciscan nuns, exiles from Germany by the Falck Laws, aboard of her were drowned I was affected by the account and happening to say so to my rector he said that he wished someone would write a poem on the subject. On this hint I set to work and, though my hand was out at first, produced one. I had long had haunting my ear the echo of a new rhythm which now I realised on paper. To speak shortly, it consists in scanning by accents or stresses alone, without any account of the number of syllables, so that a foot may be one strong syllable or it may be many light and one strong. I do not say the idea is altogether new; there are hints of it in music, in nursery rhymes and popular jingles, in the poets themselves, and, since then, I have seen it talked about as a thing possible in critics. Here are instances – '*Díng, dóng, béll*; Pússy's ín the wéll; *Whó pút* her ín? Líttle Jóhnny Thín. *Whó púlled* her óut? Little Jóhnny Stóut.' For if each line has three stresses or three feet it follows that some of the feet are of one syllable only. So too '*Óne, twó*, Búckle my shóe' *passim*. In Campbell you have 'Ánd their fléet alóng the *déep próudly* shóne' – 'Ít was tén of Ápril *mórn bý* the chíme' etc; in Shakspere 'Whý shd. *thís* désert bé?' corrected wrongly by the editors; in Moore a little melody I cannot quote; etc. But no one has professedly used it and made it the principle throughout, that I know of. Nevertheless to me it appears, I own, to be a better and more natural principle than the ordinary system, much more flexible, and capable of much greater effects. However I had to mark the stresses in blue chalk, and this and my rhymes carried on from one line into another and certain chimes suggested by the Welsh poetry I had been reading (what they call *cynghanedd*) and a great many more oddnesses could not but dismay an editor's eye, so that when I offered it to our magazine the *Month*, though at first they accepted it, after a time they withdrew and dared not print it. After writing this I held myself free to compose, but cannot find it in my conscience to spend time upon it; so I have done little and shall do less. But I wrote a shorter piece on the Eurydice, also in 'sprung rhythm', as I call it, but simpler, shorter, and without marks, and offered the *Month* that too, but they did not like it either. Also I have written some sonnets and a few other little things; some in sprung rhythm, with various other experiments – as 'outriding feet', that is parts of which do not count in the scanning (such as you find in Shakspere's later plays, but as a licence, whereas mine are rather calculated effects); others in the ordinary scanning *counterpointed* (this is counterpoint: '*Hóme to* his móther's hóuse *prívate* retúrned' and '*Bút to vánquish* by wísdom héllish wíles' etc); others, one or two, in common uncounterpointed rhythm. But even the impulse to write is wanting, for I have no thought of publishing.

I should add that Milton is the great standard in the use of counterpoint. In *Paradise Lost* and *Regained*, in the last more freely, it being an advance in his art, he employs counterpoint more or less everywhere, markedly now and then; but the choruses of *Samson Agonistes* are in my judgment counterpointed throughout; that is, each line (or nearly so) has two different coexisting scansions. But when you reach that point the secondary or 'mounted rhythm', which is necessarily a sprung rhythm, overpowers the original or conventional one and then this becomes superfluous and may be got rid of; by taking that last step you reach simple sprung rhythm. Milton must have known this but had reasons for not taking it ...

To Robert Bridges   15 February 1879

... No doubt my poetry errs on the side of oddness. I hope in time to have a more balanced and Miltonic style. But as air, melody, is what strikes me most of all in music and design in painting, so design, pattern or what I am in the habit of calling 'inscape' is what I above all aim at in poetry. Now it is the virtue of design, pattern, or inscape to be distinctive and it is the vice of distinctiveness to become queer. This vice I cannot have escaped. However 'winding the eyes' is queer only if looked at from the wrong point of view: looked at as a motion in and of the eyeballs it is what you say, but I mean that the eye winds / only in the sense that its focus or point of sight winds and that coincides with a point of the object and winds with that. For the object, a lantern passing further and further away and bearing now east, now west of one right line, is truly and properly described as winding. That is how it should be taken then.

... In the new book three poems, the 'Passer By', the 'Downs', and a sonnet beginning 'So hot the noon was' are written in a mitigated sprung rhythm. But to understand a new thing, such as this rhythm is, it is best to see it in an extreme example: you will then rather appreciate their peculiarities from it than that from them. March 7. I cannot just now get at Coleridge's preface to *Christabel*. So far as I can gather from what you say and I seem to have seen elsewhere, he was drawing a distinction between two systems of scanning the one of which is quite opposed to sprung rhythm, the other *is not, but might be developed into*, that. For though it is only a step from many popular and many literary cadences now in being to sprung rhythm and nature even without that help seems to prompt it of itself, yet the step has never, that I know of, been taken. The distinction Coleridge, as I suppose, was drawing (though it is a great abuse of terms and usage to make it by the words Accent and Quantity) is between strictly *counted rhythm*, in which, if iambic e.g., each foot has two syllables only and is an iamb; if anapaestic, each foot has three syllables and is an anapaest – this on the one hand,

and, on the other, mixed rhythm, in which feet of the same kind maybe used interchangeably, as iambs with anapaests, because both belong to *rising rhythm*, or trochees with dactyls, because both belong to *falling rhythm*. And this mixture maybe of two sorts – *equal-timed*, as in the hexameter, where the spondee is used as the alternative of the dactyl, because it is of equal length; or *logaoedic*, as when in classical and therefore strictly timed metres dactyls are mixed with trochees, which feet are of unequal length. (I leave out here all consideration of the still freer mixed lyric rhythms of antiquity.) However this last division is of little importance or meaning in English verse. It is enough that we can interchange two-syllabled with three-syllabled feet. This is freely done in ballad-measures and Coleridge does it in *Christabel*. In the more stately metres the poets of the last century as well as others before and since employ only the stricter counted rhythm, but even in the fivefoot iambic Tennyson and other modern poets often make two light syllables count for one.

This practice is founded upon an easily felt principle of *equal strengths*, as in the classic hexameter the substitution of spondees for dactyls is founded on the principle of equal lengths (or times). To go a little deeper, it supposes not only that, speaking in the abstract, any accent is equal to any other (by accent I mean *the* accent of a word) but further that each accent

148

may be considered to be accompanied by an equal quantity of slack or unaccented utterance, one, two, or more such unaccented syllables; so that wherever there is an accent or stress, there there is also so much unaccentuation, so to speak, or slack, and this will give a foot or rhythmic unit, viz. a stress with its belonging slack. But now if this is so, since there are plenty of accented monosyllables, and those too immediately preceded and followed by the accents of other words, it will come about that a foot may consist of one syllable only and that one syllable has not only the stress of its accent but also the slack which another word wd. throw on one or more additional syllables, though here that may perhaps be latent, as though the slack syllables had been absorbed. What I mean is clearest in an antithesis or parallelism, for there the contrast gives the counter-parts equal stress; e.g. 'sanguinary consequences, terrible butchery, frightful slaughter, fell swoop': if these are taken as alternative expressions, then the total strength of *sanguinary* is no more than that of *terrible* or of *frightful* or of *fell* and so on of the substantives too.

Now granting this, if the common ballad measure allows of our having (say) in a fourfoot line 'Terrible butchery, frightful slaughter' why, on principle, shd. we not say 'Terrible butchery, fell swoop' and that be four feet? or further why not 'Sanguinary consequences, terrible butchery'? – except indeed, what of course in practice and actual versewriting is important, that *consequences* is a clumsy halting word which makes the line lag. This then is the essence of sprung rhythm: *one stress makes one foot*, no matter how many or few the syllables. But all that I have said is of course shewing you the skeleton or flayed anatomy, you will understand more simply and pleasantly by verses in the flesh . . .

To Robert Bridges   26 May 1879

. . . The sestet of the Purcell sonnet is not so clearly worked out as I could wish. The thought is that as the seabird opening his wings with a whiff of wind in your face means the whirr of the motion, but also unaware gives you a whiff of knowledge about his plumage, the marking of which stamps his species, that he does not mean, so Purcell, seemingly intent only on the thought or feeling he is to express or call out, incidentally lets you remark the individualising marks of his own genius.

Sake is a word I find it convenient to use: I did not know when I did so first that it is common in German, in the form *sach*. It is the *sake* of 'for the sake of', *forsake, namesake, keepsake*. I mean by it the being a thing has outside itself, as a voice by its echo, a face by its reflection, a body by its shadow, a man by his name, fame, or memory, *and also* that in the thing by virtue of which especially it has this being abroad, and that is something distinctive, marked, specifically or individually speaking, as for a voice and echo clearness; for a reflected image light, brightness; for a shadow-casting body bulk; for a man genius, great achievements, amiability, and so on. In this case it is, as the sonnet says, distinctive quality in genius.

Wuthering is a Northcountry word for the noise and rush of wind: hence Emily Brontë's 'Wuthering Heights'.

By *moonmarks* I mean crescent shaped markings on the quill-feathers, either in the colouring of the feather or made by the overlapping of one on another ...

To R. W. Dixon   14 January 1880

... The new prosody, Sprung Rhythm, is really quite a simple matter and as strict as the other rhythm. Bridges treats it in theory and practice as something informal and variable without any limit but ear and taste, but this is not how I look at it. We must however distinguish its εἶναι and its εὖ εἶναι, the writing it somehow and the writing it as it should be written; for written anyhow it is a shambling business and a corruption, not an improvement. In strictness then and simple εἶναι it is a matter of accent only, like common rhythm, and not of quantity at all. Its principle is that all rhythm and all verse consists of feet and each foot must contain one stress or verse-accent: so far is common to it and Common Rhythm; to this it adds that the stress alone is essential to a foot and that therefore even one stressed syllable may make a foot and consequently two or more stresses may come running, which in common rhythm can, regularly speaking, never happen. But there may and mostly there does belong to a foot an unaccented portion or 'slack': now in common rhythm, in which less is made of stress, in which less stress is laid, the slack must be always one or else two syllables, never less than one and never more than two, and in most measures fixedly one or fixedly two, but in sprung rhythm, the stress being more *of* a stress, being more important, allows of greater variation in the slack and this latter may range from three syllables to none at all – *regularly*, so that paeons (three short syllables and one long or three slack and one stressy) are regular in sprung rhythm, but in common rhythm can occur only by licence; moreover may in the same measure have this range. Regularly then the feet in sprung rhythm consist of one, two, three, or four syllables and no more, and if for simplicity's sake we call feet by Greek names, taking accent for quantity, and also scan always as for rising rhythm (I call *rising rhythm* that in which the slack comes first, as in iambs and anapaests, *falling* that in which the stress comes first, as in trochees and dactyls), scanning thus, the feet in sprung rhythm will be monosyllables, iambs, anapaests, and fourth paeons, and no others. But for particular rhythmic effects it is allowed, and more freely than in common rhythm, to use any number of slack syllables, limited only by ear. And though it is the virtue of sprung rhythm that it allows of 'dochmiac' or 'antispastic' effects or cadences, when the verse suddenly changes from a rising to a falling movement, and this too is strongly felt by the ear, yet no account of it is taken in scanning and no irregularity caused, but the scansion always treated, conventionally and for simplicity, as rising. Thus the line 'She had cóme from a crúise, tráining séamen' has a plain reversed rhythm, but the scanning is simply 'She had cóme | from a crúise | tráin | ing séa | men' – that is/ rising throughout, having one monosyllabic foot and an overlapping syllable which is counted to the first foot of the next line. Bridges in the preface to his last issue says something to the effect that all sorts of feet may follow one another, an anapaest a dactyl for instance (which would make four slack syllables running): so they may, if we look at the real nature of the verse; but for simplicity it is much better to recognize, in scanning this new rhythm, only one movement, either the rising (which I choose as being commonest in English verse) or the falling (which is perhaps better in itself), and always keep to that.

In lyric verse I like sprung rhythm also to be *over-rove*, that is the scanning to run on from line to line to the end of the stanza. But for dramatic verse, which is looser in form, I should have the lines 'free-ended' and each scanned by itself.

Sprung rhythm does not properly require or allow of counterpoint. It does not require it, because its great variety amounts to a counterpointing, and it scarcely allows of it, because you have scarcely got in it that conventionally fixed form which you can mentally supply at the time when you are actually reading another one – I mean as when in reading 'Bý the wáters of life where'er they sat' you mentally supply 'By thé watérs', which is the normal rhythm. Nevertheless in dramatic verse I should sparingly allow it at the beginning of a line and after a strong caesura, and I see that Bridges does this freely in *London Snow* for instance. However by means of the 'outrides' or looped half-feet you will find in some of my sonnets and elsewhere I secure a strong effect of double rhythm, of a second movement in the verse besides the primary and essential one, and this comes to the same thing or serves the same purpose as counterpointing by reversed accents as in Milton.

But for the εὖ εἶναι of the new rhythm great attention to quantity is necessary. And since English quantity is very different from Greek or Latin a sort of prosody ought to be drawn up for it, which would be indeed of wider service than for sprung rhythm only. We must distinguish strength (or gravity) and length. About length there is little difficulty: plainly *bidst* is longer than *bids* and *bids* than *bid*. But it is not recognized by everybody that *bid*, with a flat dental, is graver or stronger than *bit*, with a sharp. The strongest and, other things being alike, the longest syllables are those with the circumflex, like *fire*. Any syllable ending in *ng*, though *ng* is only a single sound, may be made as long as you like by prolonging the nasal. So too *n* may be prolonged after a long vowel or before a consonant, as in *soon* or *and*. In this way a great number of observations might be made: I have put these down at random as samples. You will find that Milton pays much attention to consonant-quality or gravity of sound in his line endings. Indeed every good ear does it naturally more or less/ in composing. The French too say that their feminine ending is graver than the masculine and that pathetic or majestic lines are made in preference to end with it. One may even by a consideration of what the music of the verse requires restore sometimes the pronunciation of Shakspere's time where it has changed and shew for instance that *cherry* must have been *cher-ry* (like *her*, *stir*, *spur*) or that *heavy* was *heave-y* in the lines 'Now the heavy ploughman snores All with weary task foredone'. You speak of the word *over*. The *o* is long no doubt, but long *o* is the shortest of the long vowels and may easily be used in a weak place; I do not however find that Tennyson uses it so in the Ode to Memory: in the line 'Over the dewy dark [or 'dark dewy'] earth forlorn' it seems to be in a strong place . . .

To Robert Bridges   22 January 1881

. . . The little lyric 'I love my lady's eyes' is very graceful and dainty, though, as you say, unfinished in execution: 'shaded hair' I do not care for and the couplets of stanzas 1. and 2. might be bettered. The last stanza I do not understand at all. Is 'who likes' a mistake for 'who's like'? All I can make out is that the lady is recognized by her listlessness of eye in her lover's absence. I am sure it is unintelligible as it stands. I shall enclose the music to it: it is rather trifling but not more so perhaps than the words. 'Dainty-warm' is too like the *Miller's Daughter*.

I want also to enclose a recast of my *Brothers*. I sent it to Canon Dixon and he objected to the first four lines. Your objection begins *after* them. I have changed it to suit both. Do you think it improved? I know there was and fear there still is a flat where you say, but in narrative poems it needs the highest mastery to get rid of these. Only I do not see the objection to 'lost in Jack' being near the 'diver's dip': the one is a common metaphor which has almost become 'proper', I mean no longer figurative, in moral matter; the other is descriptive of a physical trick of restless impatience. The couplet you do not like in *Margaret* may be changed back to what it stood before if you like (but in the music I keep it) —

> Leaves you with your fresh thoughts can
> Feel for like the things of man.

I am setting plainchant music to it.

I do not see that the music to the Spring Odes is monotonous, rather it seems to me cheerful.

You should never say 'standpoint': 'Point of view'.

I agree that the *Eurydice* shews more mastery in art, still I think the best lines in the *Deutschland* are better than the best in the other. One may be biassed in favour of one's firstborn though. There are some immaturities in it I should never be guilty of now.

I think I remember that Patmore pushes the likeness of musical and metrical time too far — or, what comes to the same thing, not far enough: if he had gone quite to the bottom of the matter his views would have been juster. He might remember that for more than half the years music has been in the world it had perhaps *less* time than verse has, as we see in plainchant now. Sir Oozy Gore (so to say) says, and I believe him, that strict musical time, modern time, arose from dance music. Now probably verse-time arose from the dance too. The principle, whether necessary or not, which is at the bottom of both musical and metrical time is that everything shd. go by twos and, where you want to be very strict and effective, even by fours. But whereas this is insisted on and recognised in modern music it is neither in verse. It exists though and the instance Pat gives is good and bears him out. For it is very noticeable and cannot be denied that to three foot lines you can add one syllable or two syllables, which makes four feet, with pleasure, and then no more; but that to four foot lines you can comfortably add nothing. Why, but because we carry mentally a frame of fours, which being filled allows of no more? Thus –

> 'Twas when the seas did roar
> With hollow blasts of wind:
> A damsel did deplore
> All on a rock reclined –

This is in threes. Add a syllable –

> 'Twas when the seas were roaring
> With hollow blasts of wind:
> A damsel lay deploring
> All on a rock reclined –

This is three and a half and still runs smooth. Add one more –

> 'Twas when the seas were roaring, sir –

and so on with 'deploring, sir'. It flows smoothly still and is now four feet. But add one more –

> 'Twas when the seas were roaring, madam,
> With hollow blasts of wind –

And so on. *Now* it overlaps, limps, and is spoilt. And so in practice I find; for whereas in my lyrics in sprung rhythm I am strict in overreaving the lines when the measure has four feet, so that if one line has a heavy ending the next must have a sprung head (*or begin with a falling cadence*) as –

> Márgarét, áre you *gríeving*
> *Óver* Góldengróve
> [*and not e.g.* Concérning Góldengróve] unléaving? –

when it has only three I take no notice of it, for the heavy ending or falling cadence of one line does not interfere with the rising cadence of the next, as you may see in the *Brothers*. Now this principle of symmetry and quadrature has, as I think, been carried in music to stifling lengths and in verse not far enough and both need reforming; at least there is room, I mean, for a freer musical time and a stricter verse-prosody.

But about Patmore you are in the gall of bitterness.

Italics do look very bad in verse. But people will *not* understand where the right emphasis is. However they shall not be.

159

About Wyatt you are very unsatisfactory. On the fragment 'it sitteth me near' you may be right, and as likely as not it is 'sitth', for both will scan, and in Chaucer certainly *all* inflexions are open or contracted at choice. But for the whole you suggested a scanning which I believed, and believe, (no doubt without your materials for judging) to be untenable, and I think I gave reasons why I suggested another, of which you say nothing; but now, does it not meet the case? *does it not do?* Well to be sure if this one piece were all it does; but look at Wyatt, which you have before you, and see whether the principle I employed does not explain others too.

By Surrey's 'couplets of long twelves and thirteens' – a mistake for 'fourteens' – I meant the same as your '6 + 6 and 8 + 6'. It is difficult to say what makes a stanza, but I think the writer's own intention shd. decide it, which is signified by his writing or not writing in stanza-form. One certainly has a different feeling towards two lines and the same words treated as one line ...

To R. W. Dixon   1 December 1881

(the very day 300 years ago of Father Campion's martyrdom).

My Dear friend,

I am heartily glad you did not make away with, as you say you thought of doing, so warm and precious a letter as your last. It reached me on the first break or day of repose in our month's retreat; I began answering it on the second, but could not finish; and this is the third and last of them.

When a man has given himself to God's service, when he has denied himself and followed Christ, he has fitted himself to receive and does receive from God a special guidance, a more particular providence. This guidance is conveyed partly by the action of other men, as his appointed superiors, and partly by direct lights and inspirations. If I wait for such guidance, through whatever channel conveyed, about anything, about my poetry for instance, I do more wisely in every way than if I try to serve my own seeming interests in the matter. Now if you value what I write, if I do myself, much more does our Lord. And if he chooses to avail himself of what I leave at his disposal he can do so with a felicity and with a success which I could never command. And if he does not, then two things follow; one that the reward I shall nevertheless receive from him will be all the greater; the other that then I shall know how much a thing contrary to his will and even to my own best interests I should have done if I had taken things into my own hands and forced on publication. This is my principle and this in the main has been my practice: leading the sort of life I do here it seems easy, but when one mixes with the world and meets on every side its secret solicitations, to live by faith is harder, is very hard; nevertheless by God's help I shall always do so.

Our Society values, as you say, and has contributed to literature, to culture; but only as a means to an end. Its history and its experience shew that literature proper, as poetry, has seldom been found to be to that end a very serviceable means. We have had for three centuries often the flower of the youth of a country in numbers enter our body: among these how many poets, how many artists of all sorts, there must have been! But there have been very few Jesuit poets and, where they have been, I believe it would be found on examination that there was something exceptional in their circumstances or, so to say, counterbalancing in their career. For genius attracts fame and individual fame St. Ignatius looked on as the most dangerous and dazzling of all attractions. There was a certain Fr. Beschi who in Southern Hindustan composed an epic which has become one of the Tamul classics and is spoken of with unbounded admiration by those who can read it. But this was in India, far from home, and one can well understand that fame among Hindu pundits need not turn the head of an Italian. In England we had Fr. Southwell a poet, a minor poet but still a poet; but he wrote amidst a terrible persecution and died a martyr, with circumstances of horrible barbarity: this is the counterpoise in his career. Then what a genius was Campion himself! was not he a poet? perhaps a great one, if he had chosen. His History of Ireland, written in hiding and hurrying from place to place, Mr. Simpson in his Life says, and the samples prove it, shews an eloquence like Shakspere's; and in fact Shakspere made use of the book. He had all and more than all the rhetoric of that golden age and was probably the most vigorous mind and eloquent tongue engaged in theological strife then in England, perhaps in Europe. It seems in time he might have done anything. But his eloquence died on the air, his genius was quenched in his blood after one year's employment in his country. Music is more professional than poetry perhaps and Jesuits have composed and well, but none has any fame to speak of. We had one painter who reached excellence, I forget his name, he was a laybrother; but then he only painted flower pieces. You see then what is against me, but since, as Solomon says, there is a time for everything, there is nothing that does not some day come to be, it may be that the time will come for my verses.

I remember, by the by, once taking up a little book of the life of St. Stanislaus told or commented on under emblems; it was much in the style of Herbert and his school and about that date; it was by some Polish Jesuit. I was astonished at their beauty and brilliancy, but the author is quite obscure. Brilliancy does not suit us. Bourdaloue is reckoned our greatest orator: he is severe in style. Suarez is our most famous theologian: he is a man of vast volume of mind, but without originality or brilliancy; he treats everything satisfactorily, but you never remember a phrase of his, the manner is nothing. Molina is the man who *made* our theology: he was a genius and even in his driest dialectic I have remarked a certain fervour like a poet's. But in the great controversy on the Aids of Grace, the most dangerous crisis, as I suppose, which our Society ever went through till its suppression, though it was from his book that it had arisen, he took, I think, little part. The same sort of thing may be noticed in our saints. St. Ignatius himself was certainly, every one who reads his life will allow, one of the most extraordinary men that ever lived; but after the establishment of the Order he lived in Rome so ordinary, so hidden a life, that when after his death they began to move in the process of his canonisation one of the Cardinals, who had known him in his later life and in that way only, said that he had never remarked anything in him more than in any edifying priest. St.

Stanislaus Kostka's life and vocation is a bright romance – till he entered the noviceship, where after 10 months he died, and at the same time its interest ceases. Much the same may be said of St. Aloysius Gonzaga. The Blessed John Berchmans was beatified for his most exact observance of the rule; he said of himself and the text is famous among us, Common life is the greatest of my mortifications; Gregory XVI (I think) when the first steps were to be taken said of him too: At that rate you will have to canonize all the Roman College. I quote these cases to prove that show and brilliancy do not suit us, that we cultivate the commonplace outwardly and wish the beauty of the king's daughter the soul to be from within ...

To Robert Bridges   18 October 1882

Dearest Bridges,

I have read of Whitman's (1) 'Pete' in the library at Bedford Square (and perhaps something else; if so I forget), which you pointed out; (2) two pieces in the *Athenaeum* or *Academy*, one on the Man-of-War Bird, the other beginning 'Spirit that formed this scene'; (3) short extracts in a review by Saintsbury in the *Academy*: this is all I remember. I cannot have read more than half a dozen pieces at most.

This, though very little, is quite enough to give a

strong impression of his marked and original manner and way of thought and in particular of his rhythm. It might be even enough, I shall not deny, to originate or, much more, influence another's style: they say the French trace their whole modern school of landscape to a single piece of Constable's exhibited at the Salon early this century.

The question then is only about the fact. But first I may as well say what I should not otherwise have said, that I always knew in my heart Walt Whitman's mind to be more like my own than any other man's living. As he is a very great scoundrel this is not a pleasant confession. And this also makes me the more desirous to read him and the more determined that I will not.

Nevertheless I believe that you are quite mistaken about this piece and that on second thoughts you will find the fancied resemblance diminish and the imitation disappear.

And first of the rhythm. Of course I saw that there was to the eye something in my long lines like his, that the one would remind people of the other. And both are in irregular rhythms. There the likeness ends. The pieces of his I read were mostly in an irregular rhythmic prose: that is what they are thought to be meant for and what they seemed to me to be. Here is a fragment of a line I remember: 'or a handkerchief designedly dropped'. This is in a dactylic rhythm – or let us say anapaestic; for it is a great convenience in English to assume that the stress is always at the end of the foot; the consequence of which assumption is that in ordinary verse there are only two English feet possible, the iamb and the anapaest, and even in my regular sprung rhythm only one additional, the fourth paeon: for convenience' sake assuming this, then, the above fragment is anapaestic – 'or ă hánd | kérchĭef ...| . désígn | ĕdlў drópped' – and there is a break down, a designed break of rhythm, after 'handkerchief', done no doubt that the line may not become downright verse, as it would be if he had said 'or a handkerchief purposely dropped'. Now you can of course say that he meant pure verse and that the foot is a paeon – 'or ă hánd | kérchĭef désígn | ĕdlў drópped'; or that he means, without fuss, what I should achieve by looping the syllable *de* and calling that foot an outriding foot – for the result might be attained either way. Here then I must make the answer which will apply here and to all like cases and to the examples which may be found up and down the poets of the use of sprung rhythm – *if they could have done it they would*: sprung rhythm, once you hear it, is so eminently natural a thing and so effective a thing that if they had known of it they would have used it. Many people, as we say, have been 'burning', but they all missed it; they took it up and mislaid it again. So far as I know – I am enquiring and presently I shall be able to speak more decidedly – it existed in full force in Anglo saxon verse and in great beauty; in a degraded and doggrel shape in *Piers Ploughman* (I am reading that famous poem and am coming to the conclusion that it is not worth reading); Greene was the last who employed it at all consciously and he never continuously; then it disappeared – for one cadence in it here and there is not sprung rhythm and one swallow does not make a spring. (I put aside Milton's case, for it is altogether singular.) In a matter like this a thing does not exist, is not *done* unless it is wittingly and willingly done; to recognise the form you are employing and to mean it is everything. To apply this: there is (I suppose, but you will know) no sign that Whitman means to use paeons or outriding feet where these breaks in rhythm occur; it seems to me a mere extravagance to think he means people to understand of themselves what they are slow to understand even when marked or pointed out. If he does not mean it then he does not do it; or in short what he means to write – and writes – is rhythmic prose and that only. And after all, you probably grant this.

Good. Now prose rhythm in English is always one of two things (allowing my convention about scanning upwards or from slack to stress and not from stress to slack) – either iambic or anapaestic. You may make a third measure (let us call it) by intermixing them. One of these three simple measures then, all iambic or all anapaestic or mingled iambic and anapaestic, is what he in every case means to write. He dreams of no other and he *means* a rugged or, as he calls it in that very piece 'Spirit that formed this scene' (which is very instructive and should be read on this very subject), a 'savage' art and rhythm.

Extremes meet, and (I must for truth's sake say what sounds pride) this savagery of his art, this rhythm in its last ruggedness and decomposition into common prose, comes near the last elaboration of mine. For that piece of mine is very highly wrought. The long lines are not rhythm run to seed: everything is weighed and timed in them. Wait till they have taken hold of your ear and you will find it so. No, but what it *is* like is the rhythm of Greek tragic choruses or of Pindar: which is pure sprung rhythm. And that has the same changes of cadence from point to point as this piece. If you want to try it, read one till you have settled the true places of the stress, mark these, then read it aloud, and you will see. Without this these choruses are prose bewitched; with it they are sprung rhythm like that piece of mine.

Besides, why did you not say *Binsey Poplars* was like Whitman? The present piece is in the same kind and vein, but developed, an advance. The lines and the stanzas (of which there are two in each poem and having much the same relation to one another) are both longer, but the two pieces are greatly alike: just look. If so how is this a being untrue to myself? I am sure it is no such thing.

The above remarks are not meant to run down Whitman. His 'savage' style has advantages, and he has chosen it; he says so. But you cannot eat your cake and keep it: he eats his off-hand, I keep mine. It makes a very great difference. Neither do I deny all resemblance. In particular I noticed in 'Spirit that formed this scene' a preference for the alexandrine. I have the same preference: I came to it by degrees, I did not take it from him.

About diction the matter does not allow me so clearly to point out my independence as about rhythm. I cannot think that the present piece owes anything to him. I hope not, here especially, for it is not even spoken in my own person but in that of St. Winefred's maidens. It ought to sound like the thoughts of a good but lively girl and not at all like – not at all like Walt Whitman. But perhaps your mind may have changed by this.

I wish I had not spent so much time in defending the piece.

Believe me your affectionate friend

Gerard.

To Robert Bridges   26 November 1882

... The sonnet you ask about [*The Sea and the Skylark*] is the greatest offender in its way that you could have found. It was written in my Welsh days, in my salad days, when I was fascinated with *cynghanedd* or consonant-chime, and, as in Welsh *englyns*, 'the sense', as one of themselves said, 'gets the worst of it'; in this case it exists but is far from glaring. To answer in detail:

The word is *more* and is a midline rhyme to *score*, as in the next line *round* is meant in some way to rhyme to *down*. 'Rash-fresh more' (it is dreadful to explain these things in cold blood) means a headlong and exciting new snatch of singing, resumption by the lark of his song, which by turns he gives over and takes up again all day long, and this goes on, the sonnet says, through all time, without ever losing its first freshness, being a thing both new and old. *Repair* means the same thing, *renewal, resumption*. The skein and coil are the lark's song, which from his height gives the impression (not to me only) of something falling to the earth and not vertically quite but tricklingly or wavingly, something as a skein of silk ribbed by having been tightly wound on a narrow card or a notched holder or as fishing²tackle or twine¹ unwinding from a reel or winch: the laps or folds are the notes or short measures and bars of them. The same is called a score in the musical sense of score and this score is 'writ upon a liquid sky trembling to welcome it', only not horizontally. The lark in wild glee races the reel round, paying or dealing out and down the turns of the skein or coil right to the earth floor, the ground, where it lies in a heap, as it were, or rather is all wound off on to another winch, reel, bobbin, or spool in Fancy's eye by the moment the bird touches earth and so is ready for a fresh unwinding at the next flight. There is, you see, plenty meant; but the saying of it smells, I fear, of the lamp, of salad oil, and, what is nastier, in one line somewhat of Robert Browning. I felt even at the time that in the endless labour of recasting those lines I had lost the freshness I wanted and which indeed the subject demands. 'As a dare-gale skylark' is better in that respect. The peerage would be well earned. – *Crisp* means almost *crisped*, namely with notes.

To Robert Bridges   4 January 1883

... The sonnet on Purcell means this: 1–4. I hope Purcell is not damned for being a Protestant, because I love his genius. 5–8. And that not so much for gifts he shares, even though it shd. be in higher measure, with other musicians as for his own individuality. 9–14. So that while he is aiming only at impressing me his hearer with the meaning in hand I am looking out meanwhile for his specific, his individual markings and mottlings, 'the sakes of him'. It is as when a bird thinking only of soaring spreads its wings: a beholder may happen then to have his attention drawn by the act to the plumage displayed. – In particular, the first lines mean: May Purcell, O may he have died a good death and that soul which I love so much and which breathes or stirs so unmistakeably in his works have parted from the body and passed away, centuries since though I frame the wish, in peace with God! so that the heavy condemnation under which he outwardly or nominally lay for being out of the true Church may in consequence of his good intentions have been reversed. 'Low lays him' is merely 'lays him low', that is / strikes him heavily, weighs upon him. (I daresay this will strike you as more professional than you had anticipated.) It is somewhat dismaying to find I am so unintelligible though, especially in one of my very best pieces. 'Listed', by the by, is 'enlisted'. 'Sakes' is hazardous: about that point I was more bent on saying my say than on being understood in it. The 'moonmarks' belong to the image only of course, not to the application; I mean not detailedly: I was thinking of a bird's quill feathers. One thing disquiets me: *I meant* 'fair fall' to mean *fair (fortune be) fall*; it has since struck me that perhaps 'fair' is an adjective proper and in the predicate and can only be used in cases like 'fair fall the day', that is, *may the day fall, turn out, fair*. My line will yield a sense that way indeed, but I never meant it so. Do you know any passage decisive on this?

Would that I had Purcell's music here ...

To A. W. M. Baillie   14 January 1883

... My thought is that in any lyric passage of the tragic poets (perhaps not so much in Euripides as the others) there are – usually; I will not say always, it is not likely – two strains of thought running together and like counterpointed; the overthought that which everybody, editors, see (when one does see anything – which in the great corruption of the text and original obscurity of the diction is not everywhere) and which might for instance be abridged or paraphrased in square marginal blocks as in some books carefully written; the other, the underthought, conveyed chiefly in the choice of metaphors etc used and often only half realised by the poet himself, not necessarily having any connection with the subject in hand but usually having a connection and suggested by some circumstance of the scene or of the story. I cannot prove that this is really so except by a large induction of examples and perhaps not irrefragably even then nor without examples can I even make my meaning plain. I will give only one, the chorus with which Aeschylus' *Suppliants* begins. The underthought which plays through this is that the Danaids flying from their cousins are like their own ancestress Io teazed by the gadfly and caressed by Zeus and the rest of that foolery. E.g. δῖαν δὲ λιποῦσαι | χθόνα σύγχορτον Συρίᾳ φεύγομεν: the suggestion is of a herd of cows feeding next to a herd of bulls. Shortly follows a mention of Io and her story. Then comes δέξαισθ᾽ ἱκέτην | τὸν θηλυγενῆ στόλον αἰδοίῳ | πνεύματι χώρας: this alludes to the ἐπίπνοια by which Epaphus was conceived – ἀρσενοπληθῆ δ᾽ | ἑσμὸν ὑβρισ τὴν Αἰγυπτογενῆ etc: this suggests the gadfly. Perhaps what I ought to say is that the underthought is commonly an echo or shadow of the overthought, something like canons and repetitions in music, treated in a different manner, but that sometimes it may be independent of it. I find this same principle of composition in St. James' and St. Peter's and St. Jude's Epistles, an undercurrent of thought governing the choice of images used. Perhaps I spoke of this to you before . . .

To Robert Bridges   1 June 1886

. . . This leads me to say that a kind of touchstone of the highest or most living art is seriousness; not gravity but the being in earnest with your subject – reality. It seems to me that some of the greatest and most famous works are not taken in earnest enough, are farce (where you ask the spectator to grant you something not only conventional but monstrous). I have this feeling about *Faust* and even about the Divine Comedy, whereas *Paradise Lost* is most seriously taken. It is the weakness of the whole Roman literature.

To R. W. Dixon   7 August 1886

. . . Some learned lady having shewn by the flora that the season of the action in *Hamlet* is from March to May, a difficulty is raised about the glowworm's ineffectual fire in the first act, since glowworms glow chiefly from May to September. Mr. Furnival having consulted an authority learns that the grub, though not so easily found, shines nearly as bright as the fullgrown worm, that is beetle, and begins in March, and so all is saved. Does not this strike you as great trifling? Shakspere had the finest faculty of observation of all men that ever breathed, but it is ordinary untechnical observation, neither scientific nor even, like a farmer's professional, and he might overlook that point of season. But if he knew it he would likely enough neglect it. There are some errors you must not make, as an eclipse at the halfmoon or a lobster 'the Cardinal of the seas', but others do not matter and convention varies with regard to them. If I am not mistaken, there are notorious and insoluble inconsistencies in *Hamlet*, due to Shakspere's having recast the play expressly for Burbage, who was elderly, 'short, stout, and scant of breath' (or something of the sort), without taking the trouble to correct throughout accordingly – not even wishing I dare say; for no one can so conceive of Hamlet's person. Besides there are inconsistencies in the Iliad, Aeneid, Don Quixote, Three Musketeers, and so on; it is a frailty of literature. And indeed on reflection the defence makes the matter worse. For few of the audience could know that glowworms do shine, if you look well for them, in March. So that Shakspere would have been breaking Aristotle's rule, that in art likely seeming fiction is better than unlikely seeming fact.

By the by, why should Wordsworth-worship be 'a difficult thing'? It is a common one now, is it not? Not *the* common, but like soldiers in a crowd, not a numerous but a notable fact. Did you see what Lord Selborne lately said? What I suppose grows on people is that Wordsworth's particular grace, his *charisma*, as theologians say, has been granted in equal measure to so very few men since times was – to Plato and who else? I mean his spiritual insight into nature; and this they perhaps think is above all the poet's gift? It is true, if we sort things, so that art is art and philosophy philosophy, it seems rather the philosopher's than the poet's: at any rate he had it in a sovereign degree. He had a 'divine philosophy' and a lovely gift of verse; but in his work there is nevertheless *beaucoup à redire*: it is due to the universal fault of our literature, its weakness is rhetoric. The strictly poetical insight and inspiration of our poetry seems to me to be of the very finest, finer perhaps than the Greek; but its rhetoric is inadequate – seldom firstrate, mostly only just sufficient, sometimes even below par. By rhetoric I mean all the common and teachable element in literature, what grammar is to speech, what thoroughbass is to music, what theatrical experience gives to playwrights. If you leave out the embroidery (to be sure the principal thing) of for instance the *Excursion* and look only at the groundwork and stuff of the web is it not fairly true to say 'This will never do'? There does seem to be a great deal of dulness, superfluity, aimlessness, poverty of plan. I remember noticing as a boy, it was the discovery of a trade secret, how our poets treat *spirit* and its compounds as one syllable: it is, though founded really on a mistake, the mere change of pronunciation, a beautiful tradition of the poets. Wordsworth had told himself or been told this trifle: why did he not learn or someone tell him that sonnets have a natural *charpente* and structure never, or at least seldom, to be broken through? For want of knowing this his inspired sonnets, εὔμορφοι κολοσσοί, suffer from 'hernia', and combine the tiro's blunder with the master's perfection.

Believe me your affectionate friend

Gerard Hopkins.

To Coventry Patmore   7 November 1886

... I seem to have been among odds and ends of poets and poetesses of late. One poetess was Miss Kate Tynan, who lately published a volume of chiefly devotional poems, highly spoken of by reviews. She is a simple brightlooking Biddy with glossy very pretty red hair, a farmer's daughter in the County Dublin. She knows and deeply admires your Muse and said this, which appears in some way noteworthy – complaining that you are sometimes austere or bare or something like that: '*How* is it, Fr. Hopkins, that however bare it is it is always poetry?' I am at present Bridges' Muse-broker and had to send Miss Tynan an invoice of him. I am to read Miss Tynan herself when she comes, that is, as many pages as she has walked to and fro over – to say of her what one might say of any writer. Then there is a young Mr. Yeats who has written in a Trinity College publication some striking verses and who has been perhaps unduly pushed by the late Sir Samuel Ferguson (I do not know if you have read or heard of him: he was a learned antiquary, a Protestant but once an ally of Thomas Davis and the Young Ireland Party, but he withdrew from them and even suppressed some of his best poems for fear they, or he, shd. be claimed by the Nationalists of later days; for he was a poet; the *Forging of the Anchor* is, I believe, his most famous poem; he was a poet as the Irish are – to judge by the little of his I have seen – full of feeling, high thoughts, flow of verse, point, often fine imagery and other virtues, but the essential and only lasting thing left out – what I call *inscape*, that is species or individually-distinctive beauty of style: on this point I believe we quite agree, as on most: but this is a serious parenthesis). I called on his, young Yeats's, father by desire lately; he is a painter; and with some emphasis of manner he presented me with *Mosada: a Dramatic Poem* by W. B. Yeats, with a portrait of the author by J. B. Yeats, himself; the young man having finely cut intellectual features and his father being a fine draughtsman. For a young man's pamphlet this was something too much; but you will understand a father's feeling. Now this *Mosada* I cannot think highly of, but I was happily not required then to praise what presumably I had not then read, and I had read and could praise another piece. It was a strained and unworkable allegory about a young man and a sphinx on a rock in the sea (how did they get there? what did they eat? and so on: people think such criticisms very prosaic; but commonsense is never out of place anywhere, neither on Parnassus nor on Tabor nor on the Mount where Our Lord preached; and, not to quote Christ's parables all taken from real life but in the frankly impossible, as in the *Tempest*, with what consummate and penetrating imagination is Ariel's 'spiriting' put before us! all that led up and must follow the scenes in the play is realised and suggested and you cannot lay your finger on the point where it breaks down) but still containing fine lines and vivid imagery ...

To Robert Bridges 6 November 1887

... I want Harry Ploughman to be a vivid figure before the mind's eye; if he is not that the sonnet fails. The difficulties are of syntax no doubt. Dividing a compound word by a clause sandwiched into it was a desperate deed, I feel, and I do not feel that it was an unquestionable success. But which is the line you do not understand? I do myself think, I may say, that it would be an immense advance in notation (so to call it) in writing as the record of speech, to distinguish the subject, verb, object, and in general to express the construction to the eye; as is done already partly in punctuation by everybody, partly in capitals by the Germans, more fully in accentuation by the Hebrews. And I daresay it will come. But it would, I think, not do for me: it seems a confession of unintelligibility. And yet I don't know. At all events there is a difference. My meaning surely *ought* to appear of itself; but in a language like English, and in an age of it like the present, written words are really matter open and indifferent to the receiving of different and alternative verse-forms, some of which the reader cannot possibly be sure are meant unless they are marked for him. Besides metrical marks are for the performer and such marks are proper in every art. Though indeed one might say syntactical marks are for the performer too. But however that reminds me that one thing I am now resolved on, it is to prefix short prose *arguments* to some of my pieces. These too will expose me to carping, but I do not mind. Epic and drama and ballad and many, most, things should be at once intelligible; but everything need not and cannot be . . .

To Robert Bridges   10 February 1888

. . . I laughed outright and often, but very sardonically, to think you and the Canon could not construe my last sonnet [*Tom's Garland*]; that he had to write to you for a crib. It is plain I must go no farther on this road: if you and he cannot understand me who will? Yet, declaimed, the strange constructions would be dramatic and effective. Must I interpret it? It means then that, as St. Paul and Plato and Hobbes and everybody says, the commonwealth or well ordered human society is like one man; a body with many members and each its function; some higher, some lower, but all honourable, from the honour which belongs to the whole. The head is the sovereign, who has no superior but God and from heaven receives his or her authority: we must then imagine this head as bare (see St. Paul much on this) and covered, so to say, only with the sun and stars, of which the crown is a symbol, which is an ornament but not a covering; it has an enormous hat or skull cap, the vault of heaven. The foot is the daylabourer, and this is armed with hobnail boots, because it has to wear and be worn by the ground; which again is symbolical; for it is navvies or daylabourers who, on the great scale or in gangs and millions, mainly trench, tunnel, blast, and in other ways disfigure, 'mammock' the earth and, on a small scale, singly, and superficially stamp it with their footprints. And the 'garlands' of nails they wear are therefore the visible badge of the place they fill, the lowest in the commonwealth. But this place still shares the common honour, and if it wants one advantage, glory or public fame, makes up for it by another, ease of mind, absence of care; and these things are symbolized by the gold and the iron garlands. (O, once explained, how clear it all is!) Therefore the scene of the poem is laid at evening, when they are giving over work and one after another pile their picks, with which they earn their living, and swing off home, knocking sparks out of mother earth not now by labour and of choice but by the mere footing, being strongshod and making no hard-ship of hardness, taking all easy. And so to supper and bed. Here comes a violent but effective hyperbaton or suspension, in which the action of the mind mimics that of the labourer – surveys his lot, low but free from care; then by a sudden strong act throws it over the shoulder or tosses it away as a light matter. The witnessing of which lightheartedness makes me indignant with the fools of Radical Levellers. But presently I remember that this is all very well for those who are in, however low in, the Commonwealth and share in any way the Common weal; but that the curse of our times is that many do not share it, that they are outcasts from it and have neither security nor splendour; that they share care with the high and obscurity with the low, but wealth or comfort with neither. And this state of things, I say, is the origin of Loafers, Tramps, Cornerboys, Roughs, Socialists and other pests of society. And I think that it is a very pregnant sonnet and in point of execution very highly wrought. Too much so, I am afraid ...

FROM THE NOTEBOOKS

Locke. Conduct of the Understanding. § x·.. 'Who fair and softly goes steadily forward in a course that points right.' In same § 'mizmaze'.

Note on green wheat. The difference between this green and that of long grass is that first suggests silver, latter azure. Former more opacity, body, smoothness. It is the exact complement of carnation. Nearest to emerald of any green I know, the real emerald *stone*. It is lucent. Perhaps it has a chrysoprase bloom. Both blue greens.

There was neither rain nor snow, it was cold but not frosty: it had been a gloomy day with all the painful dreariness which December can wear over Clapham. M. C. came in, a little warmed by her walk. She had made a call, she had met the Miss Finlaysons, she had done some shopping, she had been round half the place and seen the nakedness of the land, and now it struck her how utterly hateful was Clapham. Especially she abominated the Berlin wool shop, where Mrs. Vandelinde and her daughter called her 'Miss' and there was a continual sound of sliding glass panels and smell of Berlin wool.

March 19, Saturday, 1864, walked to Edgeware from Hampstead and home by Hendon, stopping at Kingsbury water a quarter of an hour or so. Saw what was probably a heron: it settled on a distant elm, was driven away by two rooks, settled on a still more distant, the same thing happened, the rooks pursuing it. It then flew across the water, circled about, and flew Hampsteadwards away.

April 14. Walked with Gurney to Elsfield. Sketched E. window of church, which is in transition from decorated to perpendicular, or rather decorated with traces of perpendicularity. It had strange all its windows except the E. and two or perhaps three others. The E. had original tracery (see sketch book). These others were 3-lighted square-headed; as far as I remember the lights were lancet-shaped and cinquefoiled. The mullions were carried up to the head. The parson's son kindly let us in to see the Easter decorations. The widest and most charming views from Elsfield. A plain lies on the opposite side to Oxford with villages crowned with square church-towers shining white here and there. The lines of the fields, level over level, are striking, like threads in a loom. Splendid trees – elms, and farther on great elliptic-curve oaks. Bloomy green of larches. Standing on a high field on all sides over the hedge the horizon balanced its blue rim. The cowslips' heads, I see, tremble in wind. Noticed also frequent partings of ash-boughs.

Moonlight hanging or dropping on treetops like blue cobweb.

Also the upper sides of little grotted waves turned to the sky have soft pale-coloured cobwebs on them, the under sides green.

Note that the beaded oar, dripping, powders or sows the smooth with dry silver drops.

Poetry at Oxford.

It is a happy thing that there is no royal road to poetry. The world should know by this time that one cannot reach Parnassus except by flying thither. Yet from time to time more men go up and either perish in its gullies fluttering *excelsior* flags or else come down again with full folios and blank countenances. Yet the old fallacy keeps its ground. Every age has its false alarms.

August 1864. The poetical language lowest. To use that, which poetasters, and indeed almost everyone, can do, is no more necessarily to be uttering poetry than striking the keys of piano is playing a tune. Only, when the tune is played it is on the keys. So when poetry is uttered it is in this language. Next, Parnassian. Can only be used by real poets. Can be written without inspiration Good instance in Enoch Arden's island. Common in professedly descriptive pieces. Much of it in *Paradise Lost* and *Regained*. Nearly all *The Faery Queen*. It is the effect of fine age to enable ordinary people to write something very near it. – Third and highest, poetry proper, language of inspiration. Explain inspiration. On first reading a strange poet his merest Parnassian seems inspired. This is because then first we perceive genius. But when we have read more of him and are accustomed to the genius we shall see distinctly the inspirations and much that would have struck us with great pleasure at first loses much of its charm and becomes Parnassian. – Castalian, highest sort of Parnassian. e.g. 'Yet despair Touches me not, though pensive as a bird Whose vernal coverts winter hath laid bare.' Or 'On roses for the flush of youth etc.' Real Parnassian only written by poets and is as impossible for others as poetry, as practically it is as hard to reach the moon as the stars, but something very like it may be. Much Parnassian takes down a poet's reputation, lowers his average, as it were. Pope and all artificial schools great writers of Parnassian. This is the real meaning of an artificial poet. – The poetical language may be called language of the sacred *Plain*, Delphic. There is seemingly much Parnassian music. Same thing no doubt exists in painting.

Easter 1866. Drops of rain hanging on rails etc seen with only the lower rim lighted like nails (of fingers). Screws of brooks and twines. Soft chalky look with more shadowy middles of the globes of cloud on a night with a moon faint or concealed. Mealy clouds with a not brilliant moon. Blunt buds of the ash. Pencil buds of the beech. Lobes of the trees. Cups of the eyes, Gathering back the lightly hinged eyelids. Bows of the eyelids. Pencil of eyelashes. Juices of the eyeball. Eyelids like leaves, petals, caps, tufted hats, handkerchiefs, sleeves, gloves. Also of the bones sleeved in flesh. Juices of the sunrise. Joins and veins of the same. Vermilion look of the hand held against a candle with the darker parts as the middles of the fingers and especially the knuckles covered with ash.

March 1869. Br. Coup calls a basket a *whisket.* – One day when we were gathering stones and potsherds from the meadow Br. Wells said we were not to do it at random but 'in braids'.

March 14. About this time the weather raw and easterly, and some snow but scarcely whitening the ground. Since then (24th) dark and wet but milder.

March 27. Sun between snowstorms. In the afternoon the snow whitened the trees and grass but not the roads.

April mild but dark till the 10th, which was misty and sultry, the mist rolling in here and there by fits and quite blotting out that part of the landscape. The 11th was a little lighter. The 12th was hot and fine, so were the 13th and 14th, both beginning, especially the 14th, with fog or blight. On the 13th the cuckoo. Today (14th) lower parts of the elms out and the chestnut fans rising into shape.

Yesterday heard of Mrs. Plow's death.

April 30. Br. Wm. Kerr told me some days ago that in Australia (?) the English trees introduced had driven out the natives, mostly different kinds of gum-trees, and that he had seen a park planted with them, which were dying or dead. In particular our furze, which thrives wonderfully and grows into great hedges, has driven the native vegetation before it.

A cold May, and in fact no such hot weather as we had in April till the beginning of June and the haymaking, and then again cold winds.

Br. Wells calls a grindstone a *grindlestone.*

To *lead* north-country for to *carry* (a field of hay etc). *Geet* north-country preterite of *get*: 'he geet agate agoing'.

Trees sold 'top and lop': Br. Rickaby told me and suggested *top* is the higher, outer, and lighter wood good for firing only, *lop* the stem and bigger boughs when the rest has been lopped off used for timber.

Br. Wells calls white bryony Dead Creepers, because it kills what it entwines.

Fr. Casano's pronunciation of Latin instructive. (He is a Sicilian but has spent many years in Spain.) *Quod* he calls *c'od* and *quae hora* becomes almost *c'ora* – the *u* disappearing in a slight apostrophe; *Deus* sounds like *da-us* or *do-us*, the *e* being kept quite open; *meis* is almost a diphthong – like *mace*; *m* in *omnis* and, if I am not mistaken, final *m*s less strongly he gives the metallic nasal sound and the first syllable of *sanctus* he calls as if it were French. – Feb. 4, '70. Fr. Goldie gives long *e* like short *e* merely lengthened or even opener (the broad vowel between broad *a* and our closed *a*, the substitute for *e*, *i*, or *u* followed by *r*). Fr. Morris gives long *u* very full (*Luca*); he emphasises the semi-consonant and the vowel before it where two vowels meet – *Pio* becomes *Pī-jo* and *tuam tū-vam* (that is *pee-yo* and *too-wam*) – but in *tuum* the vowel is simply repeated. This morning I noticed Fr. Sangalli saying mass give the *m*s very slightly or bluntly.

The sunset June 20 was wine-coloured, with pencillings of purple, and next day there was rain.

June 27. The weather turned warm again two or three days ago and today is warmer still. Before that there had been cold, rain, and gloom.

Br. Sidgreaves has heard the high ridges of a field called *folds* and the hollow between the *drip*.

June 28. The cuckoo *has* changed his tune: the two notes can scarcely be told apart, that is their pitch is almost the same.

July 4. Up till the 2nd the weather gloomy. The 3rd was thick in the morning but cleared to a hazy sunlight and warm (Br. Gartlan and I in Wimbledon camp). Today is bright and hot.

July 8 and 9. Heard the cuckoo – very tuneless and wild sound.

In July some very hot days. August mild, damp, and autumnal, till near the end, when there was great heat. September began with frost and chill.

On the 8th after the Retreat the Juniors took their vows. Shortly after Fr. Fitzsimon left us suddenly and without a Goodbye and Fr. Gallwey took his place. Br. Shoolbred and Br. Anselm Gillet had left the noviceship from ill health.

1870. One day in the Long Retreat (which ended on Xmas Day) they were reading in the refectory Sister Emmerich's account of the Agony in the Garden and I suddenly began to cry and sob and could not stop. I put it down for this reason, that if I had been asked a minute beforehand I should have said that nothing of the sort was going to happen and even when it did I stood in a manner wondering at myself not seeing in my reason the traces of an adequate cause for such strong emotion – the traces of it I say because of course the cause in itself is adequate for the sorrow of a lifetime. I remember much the same thing on Maundy Thursday when the presanctified Host was carried to the sacristy. But neither the weight nor the stress of sorrow, that is to say of the thing which should cause sorrow, by themselves move us or bring the tears as a sharp knife does not cut for being pressed as long as it is pressed without any shaking of the hand but there is always one touch, something striking sideways and unlooked for, which in both cases undoes resistance and pierces, and this may be so delicate that the pathos seems to have gone directly to the body and cleared the understanding in its passage. On the other hand the pathetic touch by itself, as in dramatic pathos, will only draw slight tears if its matter is not important or not of import to us, the strong emotion coming from a force which was gathered before it was discharged: in this way a knife may pierce the flesh which it had happened only to graze and only grazing will go no deeper.

The winter was called severe. There were three spells of frost with skating, the third beginning on Feb. 9. No snow to speak of till that day. Some days before Feb. 7 I saw catkins hanging. On the 9th there was snow but not lying on the roads. On the grass it became a crust lifted on the heads of the blades. As we went down a field near Caesar's Camp I noticed it before me *squalentem,* coat below coat, sketched in intersecting edges bearing 'idiom', all down the slope: − I have no other word yet for that which takes the eye or mind in a bold hand or effective sketching or in marked features or again in graphic writing, which not being beauty nor rue inscape yet gives interest and makes ugliness even better than meaninglessness. – On the Common the snow was channelled all in parallels by the sharp driving wind and upon the tufts of grass (where by the dark colour shewing through it looked greyish) it came to turret-like clusters or like broken shafts of basalt. – In the Park in the afternoon the wind was driving little clouds of snow-dust which caught the sun as they rose and delightfully took the eyes: flying up the slopes they looked like breaks of sunlight fallen through ravelled cloud upon the hills and again like deep flossy velvet brown to the root by breath which passed all along. Nearer at hand along the road it was gliding over the ground in white wisps that between trailing and flying shifted and wimpled like so many silvery worms to and from one another.

The squirrel was about in our trees all the winter. For instance about Jan. 2 I often saw it.

Feb. 12. – The slate slabs of the urinals even are frosted in graceful sprays. [Dec. 31, 1870. I have noticed it here also at the seminary: it comes when they have been washed.]

Feb. 19 – The frost broke up. (That day also I ceased to be Porter.)

Feb. 22 – Frost again, not for long.

March 12 – A fine sunset: the higher sky dead clear blue bridged by a broad slant causeway rising from right to left of wisped or grass cloud, the wisps lying across; the sundown yellow, moist with light but ending at the top in a foam of delicate white pearling and spotted with big tufts of cloud in colour russet between brown and purple but edged with brassy light. But what I note it all for is this: before I had always taken the sunset and the sun as quite out of gauge with each other, as indeed physically they are, for the eye after looking at the sun is blunted to everything else and if you look at the rest of the sunset you must cover the sun, but today I inscaped them together and made the sun the true eye and ace of the whole, as it is. It was all active and tossing out light and started as strongly forward from the field as a long stone or a boss in the knop of the chalice-stem: it is indeed by stalling it so that it falls into scape with the sky.

The next morning a heavy fall of snow. It tufted and toed the firs and yews and went on to load them till they were taxed beyond their spring. The limes, elms, and Turkey-oaks it crisped beautifully as with young leaf. Looking at the elms from underneath you saw every wave in every twig (become by this the wire-like stem to a finger of snow) and to the hangers and flying sprays it restored, to the eye, the inscapes they had lost. They were beautifully brought out against the sky, which was on one side dead blue, on the other washed with gold.

At sunset the sun a crimson fireball, above one or two

knots of rosy cloud middled with purple. After that, frost for two days.

March 19 – St. Joseph's church opened.

March 26 – Snowstorm in morning.

In the first week of April spring began.

April 4 – In taking off my jersey of knitted wool in the dark with an accidental stroke of my finger down the stuff I drew a flash of electric light. This explains the crackling I had often heard.

On March 22 I asked the Brentford boys about a ghost story they had told me before that. At Norris's market gardens by Sion Lane there is a place where according to tradition two men (and some boys, I think) were ploughing with four horses: in bringing the plough round at the headland they fell into a covered well which they did not see and were killed. And now if you lean your ear against a wall at the place you can hear the horses going and the men singing at their work. – There are other ghosts belonging to Sion House. E.g. there is an image (of our Lady, if I remember) in a stained window which every year is broken by an unseen hand and invisibly mended again.

I was with the laybrothers that week. Br. Fitzgerald capped this story. At Singland, Co. Limerick, where he comes from, is a spring hot in winter, perishingly cold in summer, a sort of Hippocrene, called Torgha Shesheree (?), that is the Spring of the Pair, from a pair of plough-horses which were swallowed up there, the water springing up at the place. (But as the story was told me first and as it is in my notes, they were taken there to drink, the earth opened and swallowed them, and then the water sprang up at the spot: perhaps the bull is from some confusion in my account. – His account, given since, is that the plough-horses were taken there to drink, were swallowed up, and the spring much greater since: its miraculous heat and cold, I suppose, dates from then. It is ab— ⌈here I broke off months ago and cannot fill up: I must have been going to give the size or depth⌉. There are in it two broad stones, in one of which is the hoof-mark of one of the horses, and you may put your arm to the shoulder down it and feel no bottom.

He also knew a crazy woman who had dealing with 'the good people'. She would go out and bring back her apron full of straws, which appears to have had something to do with them. Her brother to stop her gave her a beating and the poor thing being sore with the blows the fairies missed her at the accustomed time. But they paid the brother for it, for they pulled him out of bed and gave him such a threshing he could not go out for a week.

Br. Byrne: – Hockey and football are much played in Ireland and the great day is Shrove Tuesday, on which the 'merits' are awarded. A player who had greatly distinguished himself at football was that day going home when in a lonely field a ball came rolling to his feet; he kicked it, it was kicked back, and soon he found himself playing the game with a fieldfull of fairies and in a place which was strange to him. The fairies would not let him go but they did their best to amuse him, they danced and wrestled before him so that he should never want for entertainment, but they could not get him to eat, for knowing that if he eat what they gave him they would have a claim upon him he preferred to starve and they for fear he should die on their hands at last put him on the right road home. On reaching home he found a pot of stirabout on the fire and had only had time to taste a ladlefull when the fairies were in upon him and began to drag him away again. He caught hold of the doorpost and called on the saints but when he came to our Lady's name they let go and troubled him no more.

Br. Byrne even gives them on the authority of some priest a theological standing ground. They are half-fallen angels who gave a part-consent to Lucifer's sin and are in probation till the last day here on earth. Their behaviour towards men comes from envy. The following story puts them in quite a devilish light. – A priest one night was driving out upon a sick call when in the dark his whip was snatched from his hand. His servant got down to look for it and found himself in the midst of the fairies. 'Father' he said, 'they're as thick as *traghneans*'. (Traghneans, however spelt, are the heads of flowering grass or of some flowering grass, often used as pipe-cleaners). The priest now began to read (say repeat, it being a dark night) some sentences from his breviary and the whip was instantly put into his hands.

'Forths' (old camps etc) belong to witches and fairies and it is very dangerous to cut or take anything from them: Br. Fitzgerald has seen a man who had gone to cut a stick in one and come back with his finger hanging off. A man was one day ploughing in a field by one of these forths and as he came up the furrow he heard a clatter of plates and knives and forks by which he guessed that the fairies were at dinner. This was enough to make him hungry and he wished for some of that dinner that they were eating. They heard him and as the plough came by again he saw a plate with knife and fork and a good dinner ready laid on the headland at the very spot where he had uttered the wish. But when he saw it he repented, for he had heard that if you eat what the fairies give you you will belong to them for good and he would not touch the food. But in an instant before he turned away one of his eyes was thrust out and lay on the plate before him and he was a one-eyed man for life because he had shuffled in dealing with the fairies.

Br. Slattery knew of a woman who had buried three children, one unbaptised, at whose wake three lights or 'candles' were seen in the yard (the grave-yard?), one weaker than the two others: these were her children's souls come to accompany hers. These 'candles' seem to be the recognised form of apparition for departed souls.

Later Br. Yates gave me the following Irish expressions – *I wouldn't put it past you* or *I wouldn't doubt you*= It is just what I should expect of you – *That you mightn't*, expression of disapproval – *Mend you* or *Sorrow mend you* or *O then the sorrow mend you*= Serves you right – *Soak it* almost = Lump it – *I haven't got it* = I don't know it – *Crackawly*= simpleton – *Johnny Magoreys*/seeds of the hip – (from Br. Considine) *Boyo'*, *Lado'* = Boy and a half etc From Br. Wood – *It puts me to the pin of my collar* = it is all I can do to bear – *As weak as a bee's knee*

Spring began in the first week of April

A day or two before May 14 the burnished or embossed forehead of sky over the sundown; of beautiful 'clear'

Perhaps the zodiacal light

May 14 Wych-elms not out till today. – The chestnuts down by St. Joseph's were a beautiful sight: each spike had its own pitch, yet each followed in its place in the sweep with a deeper and deeper stoop. When the wind tossed them they plunged and crossed one another without losing their inscape. (Observe that motion multiplies inscape only when inscape is discovered, otherwise it disfigures)

May 18 – Great brilliancy and projection: the eye

seemed to fall perpendicular from level to level along our trees, the nearer and further Park; all things hitting the sense with double but direct instress

Devotion to our Lady not only in particular but under particular attributes – There is this in Spain to our Lady of Mt. Carmel. Br. Gordon heard a man blaspheming in the street (I think in Seville): when he came to her name he said 'Against her I have nothing to say: she is not like the rest; she knows what she is about'

I was noticing his pronunciation when he read aloud. In words like *Ribadeneira* he gives to the *ei* the value of both letters, making the true diphthong between *e* and *i*. He flattens the final consonants, as *led* for *let*. The soft *g*, as in *raging*, is very noticeable: it is a Greek ξ I think, almost = *dy*

This was later. One day when the bluebells were in bloom I wrote the following. I do not think I have ever seen anything more beautiful than the bluebell I have been looking at. I know the beauty of our Lord by it. It[s inscape] is [mixed of] strength and grace, like an ash[tree]. The head is strongly drawn over [backwards] and arched down like a cutwater [drawing itself from the line of the keel]. The lines of the bells strike and overlie this, rayed but not symmetrically, some lie parallel. They look steely against [the] paper, the shades lying between the bells and behind the cockled petal-ends and nursing up the precision of their distinctness, the petal-ends themselves being delicately lit. Then there is the straightness of the trumpets in the bells softened by the slight entasis and [by] the square splay of the mouth. One bell, the lowest, some way detached and carried on a longer footstalk, touched out with the tips of the petals an oval/not like the rest in a plane perpendicular to the axis of the bell but a little atilt, and so with [the] square-in-rounding turns of the petals ... There is a little drawing of this detached bell. It looks square-cut in the original

Drought up to Corpus Xti (June 16), on evening of which day thunderstorm

Aug. 25 – A Captain Newman living in the Scilly Isles told my father he had known an old lady (she is now some years dead) who could speak Cornish. Her name was Mrs. Pendraith. I believe he knew of no other

Sept. 8 – I took my vows

Sept. 9 – To Stonyhurst to the seminary

Sept. 24 – First saw the Northern Lights. My eye was caught by beams of light and dark very like the crown of horny rays the sun makes behind a cloud. At first I thought of silvery cloud until I saw that these were more luminous and did not dim the clearness of the stars in the Bear. They rose slightly radiating thrown out from the earthline. Then I saw soft pulses of light one after another rise and pass upwards arched in shape but waveringly and with the arch broken. They seemed to float, not following the warp of the sphere as falling stars look to do but free though concentrical with it. This busy working of nature wholly independent of the earth and seeming to go on in a strain of time not reckoned by our reckoning of days and years but simpler and as if correcting the preoccupation of the world by being preoccupied with and appealing to and dated to the day of judgment was like a new witness to God and filled me with delightful fear

Oct. 20 – Laus Deo – the river today and yesterday. Yesterday it was a sallow glassy gold at Hodder Roughs and by watching hard the banks began to sail upstream, the scaping unfolded, the river was all in tumult but not running, only the lateral motions were perceived, and the curls of froth where the waves overlap shaped and turned easily and idly. – I meant to have written more. – Today the river was wild, very full, glossy brown with mud, furrowed in permanent billows through which from head to head the water swung with a great down and up again. These heads were scalped with rags of jumping foam. But at the Roughs the sight was the burly water-backs which heave after heave kept tumbling up from the broken foam and their plump heap turning open in ropes of velvet

Oct. 25 – A little before 7 in the evening a wonderful Aurora, the same that was seen at Rome (shortly after its seizure by the Italian government) and taken as a sign of God's anger. It gathered a little below the zenith, to the S.E. I think – a knot or crown, not a true circle, of dull blood-coloured horns and dropped long red beams down the sky on every side, each impaling its lot of stars. An hour or so later its colour was gone but there was still a pale crown in the same place: the skies were then clear and ashy and fresh with stars and there were flashes of or like sheet-lightning. The day had been very bright and clear, distances smart, herds of towering pillow clouds, one great stack in particular over Pendle was knoppled all over in fine snowy tufts and pencilled with bloom-shadow of the greatest delicacy. In the sunset all was big and there was a world of swollen cloud holding the yellow-rose light like a lamp while a few sad milky blue slips passed below it. At night violent hailstorms and hail again next day, and a solar halo. Worth noticing too perhaps the water-runs were then mulled and less beautiful than usual

Dec. 19 or thereabouts a very fine sunrise: the higher cloud was like seams of red candle-wax

On April 29 or thereabouts *at sunset* in the same quarter of the sky I saw, as far as I could remember it, almost the very same scape, the same colour and so on, down to a wavy wisp or rather seam above the rest – and this made by the sun shining from the West instead of the East. It was not so brilliant though

The winter was long and hard. I made many observations on freezing. For instance the crystals in mud. – Hailstones are shaped like the cut of diamonds called brilliants. – I found one morning the ground in one corner of the garden full of small pieces of potsherd from which there rose up (and not dropped off) long icicles carried on in some way each like a forepitch of the shape of the piece of potsherd it grew on, like a tooth to its root for instance, and most of them bended over and curled like so many tusks or horns or/best of all and what they looked likest when they first caught my eye/ the first soft root-spurs thrown out from a sprouting chestnut. This bending of the icicle seemed so far as I could see not merely a resultant, where the smaller spars of which it was made were still straight, but to have flushed them too. – The same day and others the garden mould very crisp and meshed over with a lace-work of needles leaving (they seemed) three-cornered openings: it looked greyish and like a coat of gum on wood. Also the smaller crumbs and clods were lifted fairly up from the ground on upright ice-pillars, whether they had dropped these from themselves or drawn them from the soil: it was like a little Stonehenge – Looking down into the thick ice of our pond I found the imprisoned air-bubbles nothing at random but starting from centres and in particular one most beautifully regular white brush of them, each spur of it a curving string of beaded and diminishing bubbles –

The pond, I suppose from over pressure when it was less firm, was mapped with a puzzle of very slight clefts branched with little sprigs: the pieces were odd-shaped and sized – though a square angular scaping could be just made out in the outline but the cracks ran deep down through the ice markedly in planes and always the planes of the cleft on the surface. They remained and in the end the ice broke up in just these pieces

1871. The spring weather began with March about

I have been watching clouds this spring and evaporation, for instance over our Lenten chocolate. It seems as if the heat by *aestus*, throes/ one after another threw films of vapour off as boiling water throws off steam under films of water, that is bubbles. One query then is whether these films contain gas or no. The film seems to be set with tiny bubbles which gives it a grey and grained look. By throes perhaps which represent the moments at which the evener stress of the heat has overcome the resistance of the surface or of the whole liquid. It would be reasonable then to consider the films as the shell of gas-bubbles and the grain on them as a network of bubbles condensed by the air as the gas rises. – Candle smoke goes by just the same laws, the visible film being here of unconsumed substance, not hollow bubbles. The throes can be perceived/ like the thrills of a candle in the socket: this is precisely to *reech*, whence *reek*. They may by a breath of air be laid again and then shew like grey wisps on the surface – which shews their part-solidity. They seem to be drawn off the chocolate as you might take up a napkin between your fingers that covered something, not so much from here or there as from the whole surface at one reech, so that the film is perceived at the edges and makes in fact a collar or ring just within the walls all round the cup; it then draws together in a cowl like a candleflame but not regularly or without a break: the question is why. Perhaps in perfect stillness it would not but the air breathing it aside entangles it with itself. The film seems to rise not quite simultaneously but to peel off as if you were tearing cloth; then giving an end forward like the corner of a handkerchief and beginning to coil it makes a long wavy hose you may sometimes look down, as a ribbon or a carpenter's shaving may be made to do. Higher running into frets and silvering in the sun with the endless coiling, the soft bound of the general motion and yet the side lurches sliding into some particular pitch it makes a baffling and charming sight. – Clouds however solid they may look far off are I think wholly made of film in the sheet or in the tuft. The bright woolpacks that pelt before a gale in a clear sky are in the tuft and you can see the wind unravelling and rending them finer than any sponge till within one easy reach overhead they are morselled to nothing and consumed –

it depends of course on their size. Possibly each tuft in forepitch or in origin is quained and a crystal. Rarer and wilder packs have sometimes film in the sheet, which may be caught as it turns on the edge of the cloud like an outlying eyebrow. The one in which I saw this was in a north-east wind, solid but not crisp, white like the white of egg, and bloated-looking

What you look hard at seems to look hard at you, hence the true and the false instress of nature. One day early in March when long streamers were rising from over Kemble End one large flake loop-shaped, not a streamer but belonging to the string, moving too slowly to be seen, seemed to cap and fill the zenith with a white shire of cloud. I looked long up at it till the tall height and the beauty of the scaping – regularly curled knots springing if I remember from fine stems, like foliation in wood or stone – had strongly grown on me. It changed beautiful changes, growing more into ribs and one stretch of running into branching like coral. Unless you refresh the mind from time to time you cannot always remember or believe how deep the inscape in things is

March 14 – Bright morning, pied skies, hail. In the afternoon the wind was from the N., very cold; long bows of soft grey cloud straining the whole heaven but spanning the skyline with a slow entasis which left a strip of cold porcelain blue. The long ribs or girders were as rollers/ across the wind, not in it, but across them there lay fine grass-ends, sided off down the perspective, as if locks of vapour blown free from the main ribs down the wind. Next day and next snow. Then in walking I saw the water-runs in the sand of unusual delicacy and the broken blots of snow in the dead bents of the hedge-banks I could find a square scaping which helped the eye over another hitherto disordered field of things. (And if you look well at big pack-clouds overhead you will soon find a strong large quaining and squaring in them which makes each pack impressive and whole.) Pendle was beautiful: the face of snow on it and the tracks or gullies which streaked and parted this well shaped out its roundness and boss and marked the slow tune of its long shoulder. One time it lay above a near hill of green field which, with the lands in it lined and plated by snow, was striped like a zebra: this Pendle repeated finer and dimmer

March 17 – In the morning clouds chalky and milk-coloured, with remarkably oyster-shell moulding. Between eleven and twelve at night a shock of earthquake

End of March and beginning of April – This is the time to study inscape in the spraying of trees, for the swelling buds carry them to a pitch which the eye could not else gather – for out of much much more, out of little not much, out of nothing nothing: in these sprays at all events there is a new world of inscape. The male ashes are very boldly jotted with the heads of the bloom which tuft the outer ends of the branches. The staff of each of these branches is closely knotted with the places where buds are or have been, so that it is something like a finger which has been tied up with string and keeps the marks. They are in knops of a pair, one on each side, and the knops are set alternately, at crosses with the knops above and the knops below, the bud of course is a short smoke-black pointed nail-head or beak pieced of four lids or nippers. Below it, like the hollow below the eye or the piece between the knuckle and the root of the nail, is a halfmoon-shaped sill as if once chipped from the wood and this gives the twig its quaining in the outline. When the bud breaks at first it shews a heap of fruity purplish anthers looking something like unripe elder-berries but these push open into richly-branched tree-pieces coloured buff and brown, shaking out loads of pollen, and drawing the tuft as a whole into peaked quains – mainly four, I think, two bigger and two smaller

The bushes in the woods and hedgerows are spanned over and twisted upon by the woody cords of the honeysuckle: the cloves of leaf these bear are some purple, some grave green. But the young green of the briars is gay and neat and smooth as if cut in ivory. – One bay or hollow of Hodder Wood is curled all over with bright green garlic

The sycomores are quite the earliest trees out: some have been fully out some days (April 15). The behaviour of the opening clusters is very beautiful and when fully opened not the single leaves but the whole tuft is strongly templed like the belly of a drum or bell

The half-opened wood-sorrel leaves, the centre or spring of the leaflets rising foremost and the leaflets dropping back like ears leaving straight-chipped clefts between them, look like some green lettering and cut as sharp as dice

The white violets are broader and smell; the blue, scentless and finer made, have a sharper whelking and a more winged recoil in the leaves

Take a *few* primroses in a glass and the instress of – brilliancy, sort of starriness: I have not the right word – so simple a flower gives is remarkable. It is, I think, due to the strong swell given by the deeper yellow middle

'The young lambs bound As to the tabour's sound'. They toss and toss: it is as if it were the earth that flung them, not themselves. It is the pitch of graceful agility when we think that. – April 16 – Sometimes they rest a little space on the hind legs and the forefeet drop curling in on the breast, not so liquidly as we see it in the limbs of foals though

Bright afternoon; clear distances; Pendle dappled with tufted shadow; west wind; interesting clouding, flat and lying in the warp of the heaven but the pieces with rounded outline and dolphin-backs shewing in places and all was at odds and at Z's, one piece with another. Later beautifully delicate crisping. Later rippling as in the drawing

April 21 – We have had other such afternoons, one today – the sky a beautiful grained blue, silky lingering clouds in flat-bottomed loaves, others a little browner in ropes or in burly-shouldered ridges swanny and lustrous, more in the Zenith stray packs of a sort of violet paleness. White-rose cloud formed fast, not in the same density – some caked and swimming in a wan whiteness, the rest soaked with the blue and like the leaf of a flower held against the light and diapered out by the worm or veining of deeper blue between rosette and rosette. Later/ moulding, which brought rain: in perspective it was vaulted in very regular ribs with fretting between: but these are not ribs; they are a 'wracking' install made of these two realities – the frets, which are scarves of rotten cloud bellying upwards and drooping at their ends and shaded darkest at the brow or tropic where they double to the eye, and the whiter field of sky shewing between: the illusion looking down the 'wagon' is complete. These swaths of fretted cloud move in rank, not in file

April 22 – But such a lovely damasking in the sky as today I never felt before. The blue was charged with simple instress, the higher, zenith sky earnest and frowning, lower more light and sweet. High up again, breathing through woolly coats of cloud or on the quains and branches of the flying pieces it was the true exchange of crimson, nearer the earth/ against the sun/ it was turquoise, and in the opposite south-western bay below the sun it was like clear oil but just as full of colour, shaken over with slanted flashing 'travellers', all in flight, stepping one behind the other, their edges tossed with bright ravelling, as if white napkins were thrown up in the sun but not quite at the same moment so that they were all in a scale down the air falling one after the other to the ground

April 27 – Went to see Sauley Abbey (Cistercian): there is little to see

Mesmerised a duck with chalk lines drawn from her beak sometimes level and sometimes forwards on a black table. They explain that the bird keeping the abiding offscape of the hand grasping her neck fancies she is still held down and cannot lift her head as long as she looks at the chalk line, which she associates with the power that holds her. This duck lifted her head at once when I put it down on the table without chalk. But this seems inadequate. It is most likely the fascinating instress of the straight white stroke

April 28 – I have never taken notice and I believe that I have never seen such size and such a noble bulk of member in the clouds as here and this day. The blue was like that blue of vase-glass, the clouds meal white, the shadow/ where it lay/ just liver-coloured and nearer the earth purplish

April 29 – I first heard the cuckoo but it has been heard before

Just caught sight of a little whirlwind which ran very fast careering across our pond. It was made by conspiring catspaws seeming to be caught in, in a whorl, to the centre. There were of course two motions, the travelling and the rotation. The circle was regular and the drawing here bad. Each tail of catspaw seemed to fling itself alive into its place in turn, so that something like the scale A B C D was very rapidly repeated all round the ring – not a complete wall at once. I saw that there was something eery, Circe-like and quick about it

May 1 – Very clear afternoon; a long chain of waxen delicately moulded clouds just tinged with yellow/ in march behind Pendle. At sunset it seemed to gather most of it to one great bale, moulded as Br. Bacon said like a brain, and I have said a bale because its knops are like the squeeze outwards of the packed stuff between the places where a network of many cords might bite into it

Found some daffodils wild but fading. You see the squareness of the scaping well when you have several in your hand. The bright yellow corolla is seeded with very fine spangles (like carnations etc) which give it a glister and lie on a ribbing which makes it like cloth of gold

May 6 – First summer-feeling day – not to last long

The banks are 'versed' with primroses, partly scattered, partly in plots and squats, and at a little distance shewing milkwhite or silver – little spilt till-fulls of silver. I have seen them reflected in green standing farmyard water

May 9 – A simple behaviour of the cloudscape I have not realised before. Before a N.E. wind great bars or rafters of cloud all the morning and in a manner all the day marching across the sky in regular rank and with equal spaces between. They seem prism-shaped, flat-bottomed and banked up to a ridge: their make is like light tufty snow in coats

This day and May 11 the bluebells in the little wood between the College and the highroad and in one of the Hurst Green cloughs. In the little wood/ opposite the light/ they stood in blackish spreads or sheddings like the spots on a snake. The heads are then like thongs and solemn in grain and grape-colour. But in the clough/ through the light/ they came in falls of sky-colour washing the brows and slacks of the ground with vein-blue, thickening at the double, vertical themselves and the young grass and brake fern combed vertical, but the brake struck the upright of all this with light winged transomes. It was a lovely sight. – The bluebells in your hand baffle you with their inscape, made to every sense: if you draw your fingers through them they are lodged and struggle/ with a shock of wet heads; the long stalks rub and click and flatten to a fan on one another like your fingers themselves would when you passed the palms hard across one another, making a brittle rub and jostle like the noise of a hurdle strained by leaning against; then there is the faint honey smell and in the mouth the sweet gum when you bite them. But this is easy, it is the eye they baffle. They give one a fancy of panpipes and of some wind instrument with stops – a trombone perhaps. The overhung necks – for growing they are little more than a staff with a simple crook but in water, where they stiffen, they take stronger turns, in the head like sheephooks or, when more waved throughout, like the waves riding through a whip that is being smacked – what with these overhung necks and what with the crisped ruffled bells dropping mostly on one side and the gloss these have at their footstalks they have an air of the knights at chess. Then the knot or 'knoop' of buds some shut, some just gaping, which makes the pencil of the whole spike, should be noticed: the inscape of the flower most finely carried out in the siding of the axes, each striking a greater and greater slant, is finished in these clustered buds, which for the most part are not straightened but rise to the end like a tongue and this and their tapering and a little flattening they have make them look like the heads of snakes

May 17 etc – I have several times seen the peacock with train spread lately. It has a very regular warp, like a shell, in which the bird embays himself, the bulge being inwards below but the hollow inwards above, cooping him in and only opening towards the brim, where the feathers are beginning to rive apart. The eyes, which lie alternately when the train is shut, like scales or gadroons, fall into irregular rows when it is opened, and then it thins and darkens against the light, it loses the moistness and satin it has when in the pack but takes another/ grave and expressive splendour, and the outermost eyes, detached and singled, give with their corner fringes the suggestion of that inscape of the flowing cusped trefoil which is often effective in art. He shivers it when he first rears it and then again at intervals and when this happens the rest blurs and the eyes start forward. – I have thought it looks like a tray or green basket or fresh-cut willow hurdle set all over with Paradise fruits cut through – first through a beard of golden fibre and then through wet flesh greener than greengages or purpler than grapes – or say that the knife had caught a tatter or flag of the skin and laid it flat across the flesh – and then within all a sluggish corner drop of black or purple oil

May 21 – Summer weather – so I wrote but there was very little of it and we have hitherto (July 5) not had one hot day but much cold and rain and so I believe it is everywhere, throughout Germany for instance. – The ashes begin to open their knots: they make strong yellow crowns against the slaty blue sky

This spring I have a good deal noticed the warp of the leaves, single or in the cluster, for instance in lime and sycomore

May 24 – At sunset and later a strongly marked moulded rack. I made out the make of it, thus – cross-hatching in fact – see April 21 and what is said there. Those may have been scarves of cloud bellying upwards but often I believe it is, as it looks in the perspective, downwards, and then they may be curds or globes and solid, geometrical solids/ that is, for all clouds are more or less cellular and hollow. Since that day and since this (May 24) I have noticed this kind of cloud: its brindled and hatched scaping though difficult to catch is remarkable when seen. I do not think it marks the direction of the flight. – Today (July 7) there has been much of this cloud and its make easily read. The solid seems given by little more than the lap or bay of a sheet.

It was a glowing yellow sunset. Pendle and all the hills rinsed clear, their heights drawn with a brimming light, in which windows or anything that could catch fluttered and laughed with the blaze – all bounded by the taught outline of a mealy blue shadow covering the valley, which was moist and giving up mist. Now where a strong shadow lay in a slack between two brows of Pendle appeared above the hill the same phenomenon I had seen twice before (one near Brussels), a wedge of light faintly edged, green on the right side, red on the left, as a rainbow would be, leaning to the right and skirting the brow of the hill with a glowing edge. It lasted as long as I looked without change – I do not know how long but between five minutes and a quarter of an hour perhaps. It had clouds it seemed to me *behind* it. Later when it was growing dark and the glow of the sunset was quite gone I noticed to the right of the spot a little – over Whalley – a rack of red cloud floating away, the red being I am persuaded a native colour, in fact it could not have been borrowed, the sun having long set and the higher clouds behind it not having it

On Whit Monday (May 29) went to Preston to see the procession. Though not very splendid it moved me. But just as it was beginning we heard the news of the murder of the hostages by the Commune at the entry of the Government troops into Paris – 64 in all, including the Archbishop, Mgr. Maret bishop of Sura, the Curé of the Madeleine, and Fr. Olivain with four other of our Fathers. It was at the same time the burning of the Tuileries and the other public buildings was carried out.

Lancashire – 'of all the wind instruments big drŏŏm fots me best'. – Old Wells directing someone how to set a wedge in a tree told him that if he would put it so and so he would 'fot it agate a riving'. – The omission of *the* is I think an extension of the way in which we say 'Father', 'government' etc: they use it when there is a relative in order to define. – They say *frae* and *aboon*

June 13 – A beautiful instance of inscape sided on the slide, that is/ successive sidings of one inscape, is seen in the behaviour of the flag flower from the shut bud to the full blowing: each term you can distinguish is beautiful in itself and of course if the whole 'behaviour' were gathered up and so stalled it would have a beauty of all the higher degree

June 17 – Solar halo at sunset: it looked bigger than usual, but this was perhaps an illusion. It was of course like a rainbow incomplete

June 19 – Two beautiful anvil clouds low on the earthline in opposite quarters, so that I stood between them

Later – Talking to James Shaw of Dutton Lee, who told us among other things that *lum* in Luke Lum means standing water and to *sail* as in Sail Wheel is to circle round. This is no tautology, for wheel is not whirlpool but only means, as I think, the double made in the water by the return current where at a spread of the stream caused by the bend or otherwise the set or stem of the river bears on one bank and sets the slacker water on its outside spinning with its friction and so working back upstream

Later – The Horned Violet is a pretty thing, gracefully lashed. Even in withering the flower ran through beautiful inscapes by the screwing up of the petals into straight little barrels or tubes. It is not that inscape does not govern the behaviour of things in slack and decay as one can see even in the pining of the skin in the old and even in a skeleton but that horror prepossesses the mind, but in this case there was nothing in itself to shew even whether the flower were shutting or opening

The 'pinion' of the blossom in the comfrey is remarkable for the beauty of the coil and its regular lessening to its centre. Perhaps the duller-coloured sorts shew it best

July 8 – After much rain, some thunder, and no summer as yet, the river swollen and golden and, where charged with air, like ropes and hills of melting candy, there was this day a thunderstorm on a greater scale – huge rocky clouds lit with livid light, hail and rain that flooded the garden, and thunder ringing and echoing round like brass, so that there is in a manner earwitness to the χαλκεον οὐρανόν. The lightning seemed to me white like a flash from a lookingglass but Mr. Lentaigne in the afternoon noticed it rose-coloured and lilac.

THE PRINCIPLE OR
FOUNDATION

THE PRINCIPLE OR FOUNDATION
An address based on the opening of The Spiritual
Exercises of St. Ignatius Loyola

The Principle or Foundation –

Homo creatus est – Creation the making out of nothing, bringing from nothing into being: once there was nothing, then lo, this huge world was there. How great a work of power!

The loaf is made with flour; the house with bricks; the plough, the cannon, the locomotive, the warship/ of iron – all of things that were before, of matter; but the world, with the flour, the grain, the wheatear, the seed, the ground, the sun, the rain; with the bricks, the clay, the earth; with the iron and the mine, the fuel and the furnace, was made from nothing. And they are made in time and with labour, the world in no time with a word. Man cannot create a single speck, God creates all that is besides himself.

But men of genius are said to create, a painting, a poem, a tale, a tune, a policy; not indeed the colours and the canvas, not the words or notes, but the design, the character, the air, the plan. How then? – from themselves, from their own minds. And they themselves, their minds and all, are creatures of God: if the tree created much more the flower and the fruit.

To know what creation is look at the size of the

world. Speed of light: it would fly six or seven times round the earth while the clock ticks once. Yet it takes *thousands of years* to reach us from the Milky Way, which is made up of stars swarming together (though as far from one another as we are from some of them), running into one, and looking like a soft mist, and each of them a million times as big as the earth perhaps (the sun is about that). And there is not the least reason to think that is anything like the size of the whole world. And all arose at a word! So that the greatest of all works in the world, nay the world itself, was easier made than the least little thing that man or any other creature makes in the world.

Why did God create? – Not for sport, not for nothing. Every sensible man has a purpose in all he does, every workman has a use for every object he makes. Much more has God a purpose, an end, a meaning in his work. He meant the world to give him praise, reverence, and service; *to give him glory.* It is like a garden, a field he sows: what should it bear him? praise, reverence, and service; it should yield him glory. It is an estate he farms: what should it bring him in? Praise, reverence, and service; it should repay him glory. It is a leasehold he lets out: what should its rent be? Praise, reverence, and service; its rent is his glory. It is a bird he teaches to sing, a pipe, a harp he plays on: what should it sing to him? etc. It is a glass he looks in: what should it shew him? With praise, reverence, and service it should shew him his own glory. It is a book he has written, of the riches of his knowledge, teaching endless truths, full lessons of wisdom, a poem of beauty: what is it about? His praise, the reverence due to him, the way to serve him; it tells him of his glory. It is a censer fuming: what is the sweet incense? His praise, his reverence, his service; it rises to his glory. It is an altar and a victim on it lying in his sight: why is it offered? To his praise, honour, and service: it is a sacrifice to his glory.

The creation does praise God, does reflect honour on him, is of service to him, and yet the praises fall short; the honour is like none, less than a buttercup to a king; the service is of no service to him. In other words *he does not need it*. He has infinite glory without it and what is infinite can be made no bigger. Nevertheless he takes it: he wishes it, asks it, he commands it, he enforces it, he gets it.

The sun and the stars shining glorify God. They stand where he placed them, they move where he bid them. 'The heavens declare the glory of God'. They glorify God, *but they do not know it*. The birds sing to him, the thunder speaks of his terror, the lion is like his strength, the sea is like his greatness, the honey like his sweetness; they are something like him, they make him known, they tell of him, they give him glory, but they do not know they do, they do not know him, they never can, they are brute things that only think of food or think of nothing. This then is poor praise, faint reverence, slight service, dull glory. Nevertheless what they can *they always do.*

But amidst them all is man, man and the angels: we will speak of man. Man was created. Like the rest then to praise, reverence, and serve God; to give him glory. He does so, even by his being, beyond all visible creatures: 'What a piece of work is man!' (Expand by 'Domine, Dominus, quam admirabile etc.... Quid est homo.... Minuisti eum paulo minus ab angelis'.) But man can know God, *can mean to give him glory.* This then was why he was made, to give God glory and to mean to give it; to praise God fréely, wíllingly to reverence him, gládly to serve him. Man was made to give, and mean to give, God glory.

I was made for this, each one of us was made for this.

Does man then do it? Never mind others now nor the race of man: do I do it? – If I sin I do not: how can I dishonour God and honour him? wilfully dishonour him and yet be meaning to honour him? choose to disobey him and mean to serve him? No, we have not answered God's purposes, we have not reached the end of our being. Are we God's orchard or God's vineyard? we have yielded rotten fruit, sour grapes, or none. Are we his cornfield sown? we have not come to ear or are mildewed in the ear. Are we his farm? it is a losing one to him. Are we his tenants? we have refused him rent. Are we his singing bird? we will not learn to sing. Are we his pipe or harp? we are out of tune, we grate upon his ear. Are we his glass to look in? we are deep in dust or our silver gone or we are broken or, worst of all, we misshape his face and make God's image hideous. Are we his book? we are blotted, we are scribbled over with foulness and blasphemy. Are we his censer? we breathe stench and not sweetness. Are we his sacrifice? we are like the sacrifice of Balac, of Core, and of Cain. If we have sinned we are all this.

But what we have not done yet we can do now, what we have done badly hitherto we can do well henceforward, we can repent our sins and begin to give God glory. The moment we do this we reach the end of our being, we do and are what we were made for, we make it worth God's while to have created us. This is a comforting thought: we need not wait in fear till death; any day, any minute we bless God for our being or for anything, for food, for sunlight, we do and are what we were meant for, made for – things that give and mean to give God glory. This is a thing to live for. Then make haste so to live.

For if you are in sin you are God's enemy, you cannot love or praise him. You may say you are far from hating God; but if you live in sin you are among God's enemies, you are under Satan's standard and enlisted there;

you may not like it, no wonder; you may wish to be elsewhere; but there you are, an enemy to God. It is indeed better to praise him than blaspheme, but the praise is not a hearty praise; it cannot be. You cannot mean your praise if while praise is on the lips there is no reverence in the mind; there can be no reverence in the mind if there is no obedience, no submission, no service. And there can be no obeying God while you disobey him, no service while you sin. Turn then, brethren, now and give God glory. You do say grace at meals and thank and praise God for your daily bread, so far so good, but thank and praise him now for everything. When a man is in God's grace and free from mortal sin, then everything that he does, so long as there is no sin in it, gives God glory and what does not give him glory has some, however little, sin in it. It is not only prayer that gives God glory but work. Smiting on an anvil, sawing a beam, whitewashing a wall, driving horses, sweeping, scouring, everything gives God some glory if being in his grace you do it as your duty. To go to communion worthily gives God great glory, but to take food in thankfulness and temperance gives him glory too. To lift up the hands in prayer gives God glory, but a man with a dungfork in his hand, a woman with a sloppail, give him glory too. He is so great that all things give him glory if you mean they should. So then, my brethren, live.

On *Principium sive Fundamentum*

'Homo creatus est' – Aug. 20 1880: during this retreat, which I am making at Liverpool, I have been thinking about creation and this thought has led the way naturally through the exercises hitherto. I put down some thoughts. – We may learn that all things are created by consideration of the world without or of ourselves the world within. The former is the consideration commonly dwelt on, but the latter takes on the mind more hold. I find myself both as man and as myself something most determined and distinctive, at pitch, more distinctive and higher pitched than anything else I see; I find myself with my pleasures and pains, my powers and my experiences, my deserts and guilt, my shame and sense of beauty, my dangers, hopes, fears, and all my fate, more important to myself than anything I see. And when I ask where does all this throng and stack of being, so rich, so distinctive, so important, come from/ nothing I see can answer me. And this whether I speak of human nature or of my individuality, my selfbeing. For human nature, being more highly pitched, selved and distinctive than anything in the world, can have been developed, evolved, condensed, from the vastness of the world not anyhow or by the working of common powers but only by one of finer or higher pitch and determination than itself and certainly than any that elsewhere we see, for this power had to force forward the starting or stubborn elements to the one pitch required. And this is much more true when we consider the mind; when I consider my selfbeing, my consciousness and feeling of myself, that taste of myself, of *I* and *me* above and in all things, which is more distinctive than the taste of ale or alum, more distinctive than the smell of walnutleaf or camphor, and is incommunicable by any means to another man (as when I was a child I used to ask myself: What must it be to be someone else?). Nothing else in nature comes near this unspeakable stress of pitch, distinctiveness, and selving, this selfbeing of my own. Nothing explains it or resembles it, except so far as this, that other men to themselves have the same feeling. But this only multiplies the phenomena to be explained so far as the cases are like and do resemble. But to me there is no resemblance: searching nature I taste *self* but at one tankard, that of my own being. The development, refinement, condensation of nothing shews any sign of being able to match this to me or give me another taste of it, a taste even resembling it.

One may dwell on this further. We say that any two things however unlike are in something like. This is the one exception: when I compare my self, my being-myself, with anything else whatever, all things alike, all in the same degree, rebuff me with blank unlikeness; so that my knowledge of it, which is so intense, is from itself alone, they in no way help me to understand it. And even those things with which I in some sort identify myself, as my country or family, and those things which I own and call mine, as my clothes and so on, all presuppose the stricter sense of *self* and *me* and *mine* and are from that derivative.

From what then do I with all my being and above all that taste of self, that selfbeing, come? Am I due (1) to chance? (2) to myself, as selfexistent? (3) to some extrinsic power?

(1) Chance in name no one acknowledges as a cause or principle or explanation of being. But to call things positive facts and refuse further explanation is to explain them by chance. What then is chance proper not chance as we use it for causes unknown or causes beside a present purpose? – Chance applies only to things possible; what must be does not come by chance and what cannot be by no chance comes. Chance then is the ἐνέργεια, the stress, of the intrinsic possibility which things have. *A* chance is an event come about by its own intrinsic possibility. And as mere possibility, passive power, is not power proper and has no activity it cannot of itself come to stress, cannot instress itself. And in fact chance existence is a selfexistence. Chance is incredible or impossible by this *a priori* consideration, but more strikingly is it incredible from experience. It is never

verified and the more examined the less is it verified, the more is it out of the question. For if it is a chance for anything at any given instant to exist and exist as so-and-so it is so for the next. These chances are equal and in any finite time it is infinitely unlikely that it should continue being and being what it was, for there are infinite instants. It is incredible then that its continued existence should be due to chance. If you say that its being is the mental flush of a string of broken existences at very small average intervals, this is incredible because monstrous. Moreover its nature should quite change, for its parts might chance elsewhere and the parts of other things here, and the variation will be infinite. The most plausible, if anything is plausible here, is that virgin matter is due to chance, other things not. But as this does not affect the present case it may be let alone. No man then can believe that his being is due to chance.

(2) Can I then be selfexistent and even in some way necessary? – This is clearly not true of my body and that crowd of being in me spoken of above, but may it be true of some part of it or something in it, *aliquid ejus*, the soul, the mind and its consciousness?

The mind and all my being is finite. This is plain in its outward and inward operations. In its outward, for there is a resistance in the body and things outside the body which it cannot overcome; there is a degree of effort, pain, weariness to which it yields. And in the inward; it has a finite insight, memory, grasp of apprehension, power of calculation, invention, force of will.

Nothing finite can exist of itself. For being finite it is limited and determined in time and space, as the mind is limited and determined to particular dates of time and place by the body. And apart from the body it is determined. I say apart from the body because it may be maintained that the mind has no bound from space nor even from time, for it may exist after death and may have existed before birth. Nevertheless it is finite in its own being, as said above, and determined. Its faculties compared one with another and compared with those of other minds are determined; they might be more, they might be less, they might be otherwise; they are then determined and distinctive. It is plain it might have more perfection, more being. Nevertheless the being it has got has a great perfection, a great stress, and is more distinctive and higher selved, than anything else I see, except other such minds, in nature. Now to be determined and distinctive is a perfection, either self-bestowed or bestowed from without. In anything finite it cannot be self-bestowed; nothing finite can determine its own being, I mean its being as a whole; nothing finite can determine what itself shall, in the world of being, be. For to determine is a perfection, greater than and certainly never less than, the perfection of being determined. It is a function of a nature, even if it should be the whole function, the naturing, the selving of that nature. It always in nature's order is after the nature it is of. Nothing finite then can either begin to exist or eternally have existed of itself, because nothing can in the order of time or even of nature act before it exists or exercise function and determination before it has a nature to 'function' and determine, to selve and instress, with; how much less then when the very determination is what the determiner itself is to be and the selving what its self shall be like! And this is above all true of that inmost self of mine which has been said to be and to be felt to be, to taste, more distinctive than the taste of clove or alum, the smell of walnutleaf or hart'shorn, more distinctive, more selved, than all things else and needing in proportion a more exquisite determining, selfmaking, power.

But is it as a last alternative possible that, though neither my body nor the faculties and functions of my soul exist of themselves, there should be one thing in the soul or mind, as if compounded or selved-up with these, which does? a most spiritual principle in some manner the form of the mind as the mind or the soul is said to be of the body; so that my mind would be one selving or pitch of a great universal mind, working in other minds too besides mine, and even in all other things, according to their natures and powers and becoming conscious in man. And this would be that very/ distinctive self that was spoken of. Here we touch the *intellectus agens* of the Averrhoists and the doctrine of the Hegelians and others.

Whether anything of this sort can be true or not, alike I find that I myself can not be selfexistent. I may treat the question from the side of my being, which is said to be compounded, selved-up, or identified with this universal mind, or from the side of the universal mind itself. And first from my side.

The universal mind being identified not only with me but also with all other minds cannot be the means of communicating what is individual in me to them nor in them to me. I have and every other has, as said above, my own knowledge and powers, pleasures, pains, merit, guilt, shame, dangers, fortunes, fates: we are not chargeable for one another. But these things and above all my shame, my guilt, my fate are the very things in feeling, in tasting, which I most taste that selftaste which nothing in the world can match. The universal cannot taste this taste of self as I taste it, for it is not to it, let us say/ to him, that the guilt or shame, the fatal consequence, the fate, comes home; either not at all or not altogether. If not at all, then he is altogether outside of my self, my personality/ one may call it, my *me*. If not altogether, if for instance there is something done or willed which I am wholly chargeable with and answerable for and he only so far as I am a part of him, a function or selving of his, then only so far is he answerable and chargeable, and this difference may make the difference of mortal and venial sin and of a happy or unhappy fate. Put it thus: suppose my little finger could have a being of its own, a personal being, without ceasing to be my finger and my using it and feeling in it; if now I hold it in the candleflame the pain of the burning, though the selfsame feeling of pain, experienced by me in my finger and by my finger in itself, will be nevertheless unlike in us two, for to my finger it is the scorching of its whole self, but to me the scorching only of one finger. And beyond this, taking it morally, if I have freely put my finger into the flame and the finger is unwilling, but unable to resist, then I am guilty of my folly and self-mutilation, but my finger is innocent; if on the other hand my finger is willing, then it is more guilty than I, for to me the loss of a finger is but mutilation, but to my finger itself it is selfmurder. Or if again it were selfsacrifice the sacrifice would be nobler in the finger, to which it was a holocaust, than in me, in whom it was the consuming of a part only. Though then I most intimately share my finger's feeling of pain, for indeed it is to me and to it one and the same, I do not share its feeling of self at all and share little, if I share any, of its guilt or merit, fortune and fate.

So then the universal mind is outside of my inmost self and not within it; nor does it share my state, my moral standing, or my fate. And for all that this universal being may be at work in mine it leaves me finite: *I* am selfexistent none the more for any part the selfexistent plays in me.

And the same conclusion follows if I look at the matter from the other side, that of the universal mind or being itself. For (1) the universal being too must have its self, its distinctive being, and distinctive more than mine. For if this is what I find myself to have above all other things I see, except only my peers in nature, other men, this self, in its taste to me so distinctive, how much more this greater being! Now if it, or he, has the same intimate feeling, consciousness, of all that goes on in me as I have of what goes on in my finger, so that even I were to him like a part or member, or not to speak of parts or members in what is infinite, as a feature or a selving, yet as my self was outside my finger's in the case supposed above and its self outside mine so must this infinite being's self be outside of mine as clearly as mine is outside of his: he must be able to think, mean, and say *I* and *me* as much as I am and when he says them he does not mean me who write this. Then too if, as said above, he does not (or not in the same degree) bear my guilt or merit or feel my shame, neither do I his: if e.g. it is ambition in him to want to be identified with or compounded or selved-up with all things, that is not my case nor my ambition, for I am compounded only with him and that by no choice of mine; if it is charity in him so to impart him self to all, that is not my case nor my merit either. And more generally (2) his *inlaw*, the law of his being is unlike mine, as the Ten of Hearts is unlike any one of the hearts in it: it is many or made of many, each of them is one. In fact his very composition with me, being a sample of his composition with other things, all things, makes him unlike me or any other one thing. If X is compounded with A, B, C, D etc so as to give AX, BX, CX, DX etc, then X has its being in a series, which is its inlaw, but A and B or AX and BX have not. And if it has besides a simple being X besides the series, that makes the matter no better. Whether then the universal mind by *me* and *myself* means his Being X or his Being in the shape of the series AX, BX etc he has another self than mine, which is, say, CX; either way self tastes differently to him and to me.

For, to speak generally, whatever can with truth be called a self – not merely in logic or grammar, as if one said Nothingness itself –, such as individuals and persons must be, is not a mere centre or point of reference for consciousness or action attributed to it, everything else, all that it is conscious of or acts on being its object only and outside it. Part of this world of objects, this object-world, is also part of the very self in question, as in man's case his own body, which each man not only feels in and acts with but also feels and acts on. If the centre of reference spoken of has concentric circles round it, one of these, the inmost, say, is its own, if óf it, the rest are tó it only. Within a certain bounding line all will be self, outside of it nothing: with it self begins from one side and ends from the other. I look through my eye and the window and the air; the eye is my eye and of me and me, the windowpane is my windowpane but not of me nor me. A self then will consist of a centre *and* a surrounding area or circumference, of a point of reference *and* a belonging field, the latter set out, as surveyors etc say, from the former; of two elements, which we may call the inset and the outsetting or the display. Now this applies to the universal mind or being too; it will have its inset and its outsetting; only that the outsetting includes all things, with all of which it is in some way, by turns, in a series, or however it is, identified. But then this is an altogether different outsetting from what each of those very things to its own particular self has. And since self consists in the relation the inset and the outsetting bear to one another, the universal has a relation different from everything else and everything else from everything else, including the universal, so that the self of the universal is not the self of anything else. In other words the universal is not really identified with everything else nor with anything else, which was supposed; that is/ there is no such universal.

In shewing there is no universal a true self which is 'fetched' or 'pitched' or 'selved' in every other self, I do not deny that there is a universal really, and not only logically, thus fetched in the universals, but either it is selfless and they Selves, as may be the case in Man, or else it may be a true Self and they like its members only and not true Selves, something like which I am inclined to believe the species and individual in the brutes, or at least that the specific form, the form of the whole species, is nearer being a true Self than the individual. But these universals are finite only.

In the case of such a universal as humanity these questions would arise: *first* of the attributes – say the merit or guilt – of each member, each individual by and to itself; *next* those of the universal collectively, the average morality; *thirdly* those of each member considered as a pitch of the universal and so of the universal morality and the degree in which each agrees or disagrees with, avows or disavows this average morality.

Neither do I deny that God is so deeply present to everything ('Tu autem, O bone omnipotens, eras superior summo meo et interior intimo meo') that it would be impossible for him but for his infinity not to be identified with them or, from the other side, impossible but for his infinity so to be present to them. This is oddly expressed, I see; I mean/ a being so intimately present as God is to other things would be identified with them were it not for God's infinity or were it not for God's infinity he could not be so intimately present to things.

There is another proof that the universal being cannot be selved in or identified with all other things. Either the universal is selved not only in this world of things but in all possible ones or only in this one. If in all possible worlds then there is no difference between possible and actual and all possible and 'incompossible', incompatible, frames of being exist together or *are* together, for what coexist with a third thing (or are as true as a third thing) coexist with (or are as true as) one another. But this is absurd. Only then is this. Then this world must have been determined by the universal being out of all possible worlds, for, as shewn above, it could not determine its own being or determine itself into being. If so the universal exercises choice, is selfdetermining. But this is a great proof of self. It has then a self independent of its supposed selving in other things or, in other words it is not selved in or identified with other things.

No thing then, including myself, is in any sense selfexistent except this great being.

(3) The third alternative then follows, that I am due to an extrinsic power.

(Remark that the assumption in no. 2 is to assume in oneself a hypostatic union.) – Aug. 12 1882

From On *Prima Hebdomada. Examen Conscientiae Generale*

A person is defined a rational (that is/ intellectual) supposit, the supposit of a rational nature. A supposit is a self. Self is the intrinsic oneness of a thing, which is prior to its being and does not result from it *ipso facto*, does not result, I mean, from its having independent being; for accidental being, such as that of the broken fragments of things or things purely artificial or chance 'installs', has no true and intrinsic oneness or true self: they have independent existence, that is/ they exist distinct from other things and by or in themselves, but the independence, the distinctness, the self is brought about artificially; naturally ivory is a tusk, the sphere of ivory meant to be a billiard ball is artificially made so, by turning. Now a bare self, to which no nature has yet been added, which is not yet clothed in or overlaid with a nature, is indeed nothing, a zero, in the score or account of existence, but as possible it is positive, like a positive infinitesimal, and intrinsically different from every other self.

For in the world, besides natures or essences or 'inscapes' and the selves, supposits, hypostases, or, in

the case of rational natures, persons/ which wear and
'fetch' or instance them, there is still something else –
fact or fate. For let natures be A, B, ... Y, Z and
supposits or selves $a, b, ... y, z$: then if a is capable of A, B,
... Y, Z (singly or together) and receives, say, A, if b
capable of the same receives also A, and if c capable of
the same receives M, so that we have aA, bA, cM, these
combinations are three arbitrary or absolute facts not
depending on any essential relation between a and A, b
and A, or c and M but on the will of the Creator. Further,
a and b are in the same nature A. But a uses it well and is
saved, b ill and is damned: these are two facts, two fates/
not depending on the relation between a and b on the
one hand and A on the other. Now as the difference of
the facts and fates does not depend on A, which is the
same for both, it must depend on a and b. So that selves
are from the first intrinsically different.

But this intrinsic difference, though it always exists,
cannot appear except in a rational, to speak more to the
point/ in a free/ nature. Two eggs precisely alike, two
birds precisely alike/ will behave precisely alike: if they
had been exchanged no difference would have been
made. It is the self then that supplies the determination,
the difference, but the nature that supplies the exercise,
and in these two things freedom consists. This is what I
have before somewhere worked out in a paper on
freedom and personality and I think I used the terms

freedom of pitch and *freedom of play*: they are good at all events and the two together express moral freedom.

Now if self begins to manifest its freedom with the rise from an irrational to a rational nature it is according to analogy to expect it will manifest more freedom with further rise in nature. Accordingly we find a more tremendous difference in fate between the good and the fallen angels than between good and bad or even saved and lost men. And this reasoning is of wide application. But the scale of natures is infinite up towards the divine. Now as the evil of venial sin is that if only the quantity of the matter were increased or the consent more perfect it would be mortal: so mortal sin itself seems to take its malice from an ideal sin worse and blacker than any that ever were or could be committed, in this way: he who breaks one commandment is guilty of all, St. James says, because he breaks *God's commandment*; murder is a mortal sin against God because if you will murder man you may come, as Caiphas and Pilate did, to *murder the man who is God*; and in general, if only God could be put into the position: the mortal sinner would have his way with him (the men of Sodom, Judas, and Caiphas are three typical cases), spoil him, sell him, or make away with him. Or to put it another way, if the sinner defiles God's image so he might God's person if he could; if he takes the limbs of Christ and makes them members of a harlot so he would

Christ; if he could be, as Christ was, 'in the form of God' he would make God sin and do the deeds 'of a slave'. Sin seems to reach up to an, as it were, preposterous and wicked godhead: in this lies the infinity of its malice, so far as that is infinite, and the realising this is that pain, in the pain or penalty of loss, which is even relieved by the realising, in the pain of sense, the very act of sin which merited it.

But if this is so and guilt can grow greater with increase in perfection of nature how is it that every being might, if God chose, be saved? For it would appear that with higher opportunities Judas and Satan might have sinned more, not less. Here then we must consider that as there is a scale of natures, ranging from lower to higher, which height is no advantage at all to the evil self, the self which will give nature, and the higher the nature the more, a pitch to evil; so also there is a scale or range of pitch which is also infinite and terminates upwards in the directness or uprightness of the 'stem' of the godhead and the procession of the divine persons. God then can shift the self that lies in one to a higher, that is/ better, pitch of itself; that is/ to a pitch or determination of itself on the side of good. But here arises a darker difficulty still; for how can we tell that each self has, in particular, any such better self, any such range from bad to good? In the abstract there is such a range of pitch and conceivably a self to be found, actually or possibly, at each pitch in it, but how can *each* self have all these pitches? for this seems contrary to its freedom; the more so as if we look at the exhibition of moral freedom in life, at men's lives and history, we find not only that in the same circumstances and seemingly with the same graces they behave differently, not only they do not range as fast from bad to good or good to bad one as another, but, even what is most intrinsic to a man, the influence of his own past and of the preexisting disposition of will with which he comes to action seems irregular and now he does well, now he sins, bids fair to be a sinner and becomes a saint or bids fair to be a saint and falls away, and indeed goes through vicissitudes of all sorts and changes times without number.

This matter is profound; but so far as I see this is the truth. First, though self, as personality, is prior to nature it is not prior to pitch. If there were something prior even to pitch, of which that pitch would be itself the pitch, then we could suppose that that, like everything else, was subject to God's will and could be pitched, could be determined, this way or that. But this is really saying that a thing is and is not itself, is and is not A, is and is not. For self before nature is no thing as yet but only possible; with the accession of a nature it becomes properly a self, for instance a person: only so far as it is prior to nature, that is to say/ so far as it is a definite self, the possibility of a definite self (and not merely the possibility of a number or fetch of nature) it is identified with pitch, moral pitch, determination of right and wrong. And so far, it has its possibility, as it will have its existence, from God, but not so that God makes pitch no pitch, determination no determination, and difference indifference. The indifference, the absence of pitch, is in the nature to be superadded. And when nature is superadded, then it cannot be believed, as the Thomists think, that in every circumstance of free choice the person is of himself indifferent towards the alternatives and that God determines which he shall, though freely, choose. The difficulty does not lie so much in his being determined by God and yet choosing freely, for on one side that may and must happen, but in his being supposed equally disposed or pitched towards both at once. This is impossible and destroys the notion of freedom and of pitch.

Nevertheless in every circumstance it is within God's power to determine the creature to choose, and freely choose, according to his will; but not without a change or access of circumstance, over and above the base act of determination on his part. This access is either of grace, which is 'supernature', to nature or of more grace to grace already given, and it takes the form of instressing the affective will, of affecting the will towards the good which he proposes. So far this is a necessary and constrained affection on the creature's part, to which the *arbitrium* of the creature may give its avowal and consent. Ordinarily when grace is given we feel first the necessary or constrained act and after that the free act on our own part, of consent or refusal as the case may be. This consent or refusal is given to an act either hereafter or now to be done, but in the nature of things such an act must always be future, even if immediately future or of those futures which arise in acts and phrases like 'I must ask you' to do so-and-so, 'I wish to apologise', 'I beg to say', and so on. And ordinarily the motives for refusal are still present though the motive for consent has been strengthened by the motion, just over or even in some way still working, of grace. And therefore in ordinary cases refusal is possible not only physically but also morally and often takes place. But refusal remaining physically possible becomes morally (and strictly) impossible in the following way.

Besides the above stated distinction of freedom of pitch and freedom of play there is a third kind of freedom still to be considered, *freedom of field*. (This is the natural order of the three: freedom of pitch, that is/self-determination, is in the chooser himself and his choosing faculty; freedom of play is in the execution; freedom of field is in the object, the field of choice.) Thus it is freedom of play to be free of some benevolent man's purse, to have access to it at your will; it is freedom of pitch to be allowed to take from it what you want, not to be limited by conditions of his imposing; it is freedom of field to find there *more than one coin to choose from.* Or it is freedom of pitch to be able to choose for yourself which of several doors you will go in by; it is freedom of play to go unhindered to it and through the one you choose; but suppose all were false doors or locked but the very one you happened to choose and you do not know it, there is here wanting freedom of field.

INDEX OF FIRST LINES